The Book of Affirmations

The Book of Affirmations

Sharon Elaine

Deepak Chopra endorses "The Book of Affirmations"! Famed author, doctor and metaphysician, Deepak Chopra, has provided a personal quote for The Book of Affirmations.

"Sharon's affirmations will undoubtedly help anyone on their spiritual journey."

Deepak Chopra,
Author, The Seven Spiritual Laws of Success

THANKS DEEPAK!!!

<u>*Reviews for The Book of Affirmations*</u>

"I really like this book. If you are like me, it can be a real challenge to come up with a positive affirmation when you are feeling low, confused or filled with an emotion that is threatening your peace. Sharon Elaine's book is divided into many different subject areas and filled with a variety of affirmations in each area. I have used this book a lot and think that it is a great tool for changing destructive feelings/beliefs into constructive ones. I highly recommend this book!"

Tami Coyne, author of "Your Life's Work: A Guide to Creating a Spiritual and Successful Work Life" and co-author of "The Spiritual Chicks Question Everything: Learn to Risk, Release and Soar"

••

"This is an easy book to use, as it has all kinds of subjects for the affirmations. I think it's helpful. I've been down lately, and repeating these sentences has helped my attitude a lot."

Reader from New York, NY

••

"Even the most secure of us let doubts creep into our everyday lives. Sharon Elaine has provided us with a handy source of reinforcing the positive attitudes we work so hard to acquire. Her concise statements allow the reader to get a quick "pick-me-up," and may even be used in meditation."

Reader from Chicago, IL

••

"Life can be stressful, everyone is too busy doing a million things at once and it's easy to get bogged down and depressed. We need to take time out for ourselves, time to relax and take care of ourselves. In "The Book of Affirmations" Sharon Elaine reinforces this idea in a big way! This book gives you a detailed list of all different types of affirmations to bring you back into a happier, more peaceful place.
ANYONE WHO ENJOYS AFFIRMATIONS, MEDITATION, NEW AGE PRINCIPLES, ETC., WILL LOVE THIS BOOK!"

Reader from California, USA

• •

"A friend gave me "The Book of Affirmations" as a gift shortly after my brother passed away. I was sinking fast and they said that the book had been a tremendous help to them and I should give it a try. To give you just a little background... my brother was only 35 and one of my best friends. It was a year ago today. This has been a hardship on my life that is indescribable. The fact that I am able to write a review about this time in my life should indicate to you how remarkable this book truly is. There were times I didn't think I could go on... times I felt I didn't want to... reading these most uplifting and spiritual affirmations kept me from going over the edge on many occasions. I carry the book with me wherever I go. If I feel myself slipping, I just take it out and read. Sometimes I go to specific areas within the book - sometimes I just open it and read. Either way, it has saved me on more than one occasion. Sharon Elaine truly has "A Gift from God" and I, for one, am grateful she has chose to share it with us - not only for myself, but for my husband and our three children."

Reader from Okinawa, Japan

• •

"Caring for others begins with caring for the self. Sharon's book is a delightful reminder that we cannot do our best work in this world if we are not fully-fortified and confident about our abilities to move in and upon it. Laid out in a way that recognizes that we don't always have the time we need to regroup during a busy day and allows the reader to quickly find words of encouragement when they are needed, the book can also be enjoyed in a longer read--soaked in as a gift to oneself during those precious times of stillness. When I am angry, or blue, tired, or frustrated, whenever my ability to give love and support is challenged by others who wish to boost their egos by eroding my sense of self-worth or by the pressures of my job or my family, I open Sharon's book and find tools for rejuvenation."

Reader from Wisconsin, USA

•••

"This book is just wonderful! Anytime I get down in life, this book always helps me! Thanks Sharon for such an inspiring, helpful book!"

Reader from email

•••

"This is more than just a book read once and put on a shelf. The use of positive affirmations has become a continuous practice for me and has helped me change my perception, which consequently, has improved my life. It is very simple to locate the category a current emotion is related to, and as the appropriate affirmations are read, I can feel an attitude shift in myself almost immediately. Becoming familiar with affirmations, I started being aware of all the negative words I heard throughout the day. I have found myself contradicting them with positive affirmations.

"Thank you, Sharon, for writing this book so I could give it to myself! What a great book to keep with you at all times, especially when those negative thoughts come creeping in. I really love how they are categorized so you can look something up in a hurry! If everyone had this book and took time each day to read and act on the contents, there would be so much universal positive energy flowing that our world would begin a great healing process."

Reader from Utah, USA

"[The Book of Affirmations] has specific examples, really helpful book! I keep it with me at all times for a quick uplift. I'm using more and more affirmations than ever! Thanks!"

Reader from email

"This is a truly wonderful book…a book that belongs in everyone's collection…filled with lots of inspiration and spirit. It truly says the things to you that you need and have been wanting to hear for a very long time. As you sit and read, and read, for this is a hard book to put down once you open a page, you hear yourself agreeing with everything you read. The words flow easily and comfortably into your mind, making it easy to accept these words as your own. This is the kind of book that doesn't belong on your bookshelf, but on your headboard or under your pillow even, to have right there when you go to bed at night and wake in the morning. Read a few pages and start your days with a much more positive attitude and outlook on life. To be honest with you this would be a great book to carry around with you all day."

Reader from online review

Sharon has a web site with many areas of interest, including:

- Sharon's books and CDs

- Sharon's Bio, Blog and Newsletter

- Sign-up area to join Sharon's Affirmation Focus Groups

- Sharon's *Ready, Click, Win!* book, which tells how to enter online sweepstakes

Sharon's web site is:

www.unleashedminds.com

I dedicate this book to my wonderful parents:

June and Elmer

To my sisters:

Pam and Debbie

to my wonderful children:

Becky, Justin and Nick

and to my sweet soulmate:

Kevin

TABLE OF CONTENTS

ACKNOWLEDGMENTS

Special thanks to some of the people who make motivational and/or metaphysical study their life work. I've enjoyed (and been inspired by) your work for many years. Thank you so much for coming into my consciousness.

Deepak Chopra, Anthony Robbins, Louise Hay, Jan Kabat-Zinn, Richard Bach, Bartholomew, James Redfield, Wayne Dyer, Marianne Williamson, Abraham-Hicks, SAM, Pema Chodron, And many, many more!

PERSONAL ACKNOWLEDGEMENTS

My wonderfully incredible children I wish to thank the most. They have lived under the same roof(s) with me their whole lives, have ridden with me on my roller coaster of a life, and have still managed to hold onto their individuality and genuine goodness. They are the brightest, funniest, most enlightened, most tender, caring children I could ever hope to have in my life. They are always eager to help, and genuinely care about each other and the future of the world. Rebecca and Justin are my 22-year old twins, and Nicholas is my 14-year old son. I love, you, kids, you're the lights of my life. I cherish and respect you more than words can say; I'm honored to be your Earth mother.

My parents, Elmer and June Childress, deserve many thanks for supporting me and believing in me throughout my life. They've been married 58 years, are devoted to one another, and equally devoted to their children and grandchildren. I love you, Mom and Dad. Thanks for the wonderful role models that you are and for supporting me through this project, and many, many others.

My sisters (Pam Childress and Debbie Childress), live in separate parts of California. I'm so honored to have them as my big sisters. We've lived many miles apart for a long time, yet have remained much closer than many sisters who live within the same city. They are both so gifted. Penny, I love you, sweetie, and you have the singing voice of many angels. Daaahhbie, Daahhbie, you're such a talented musician and songwriter, and I love you. Sorry, girls, for all the times you've had to put up with the antics of your kid sister (remember the wrong car at the drive-in?).

My fabulous cousin Felicia Oswalt resides in Arkansas. She's the one I used to dress exactly like, and wanted to be like when I grew up. This amazing, high-positive-energy woman always keeps her sense of humor, and her full, beautiful heart. She is the author of the famous line "Do anything you want in life, because they'll never see you again anyway!" Flee, I love you, girlfriend.

My sensational friend Sherri Harsh, has always bent over backwards for her friends. Granted, I have to put up with her breathtaking beauty, incredible intelligence and scathing wit, but she's worth it. She loves me for who I am, and we refuse to give up our friendship, even in the midst of our busy lifestyles. She lives with husband, Chuck, and her children Kalani, Kory and Kitari. Sherri, I love you, even though you keep getting me kicked out of those fast food restaurants. I LYLASS always.

And last, but not least, my sweet soul mate Kevin Schuhart. He means more to me than I can possibly write within these words. He loves me for exactly who I am (quirks and all). He is my best friend and someone I have tremendous fun with. He's open-minded, loving and most of all supportive… through allll of these projects I keep getting myself into. You're my rock and I don't want to think of living without you. We are a perfect team. I love you, sweet "Ricky"… Love, "Lucy"

Many thanks to: Anita Hillin, Nathan Rankin (in spirit); Shannon…wherever you are; Shari Hauck; Ken Adi-Ring, Joyce Slater; Iris Smithers, Tami Coyne; Helen Gray; Dottie Pendleton; Angel Hughes; Bob Schroeder; Bill and Shirley Schuhart; Dave and Stephanie Schuhart; Marilyn and Felix Childress, Neo and Nathan (our puppies); my students that I teach at Fox Valley Technical College; and all of the wonderful, amazing women on my Freebie/Sweepstakes online discussion board.

PREFACE

Once upon a time .... I started paying attention to my thoughts. I found I was processing a lot of negative self-talk. At first, this realization was distressing, as I felt powerless over the information that was permeating my mind and my life.

But then I began to take a few of those negative thoughts, just a few at first, and turn them around. I wasn't very confident when I began this experiment, so I only allowed myself to alter a few each day. What I found was that when I successfully altered my negative thought patterns into positive ones, I began feeling stronger, happier, and more in control of my life.

After altering my thoughts more frequently, and with continued success, I decided it would be a good idea to begin writing some affirmations down. Then one day, while I was meditating, the idea for this book revealed itself to me. It's very important for me to help others understand that anyone and everyone can use affirmations with a great deal of success.

Use this book any way you please, of course. My idea was to take all kinds of positive statements and separate them into categories for different needs. The affirmations may be read in order, or at random. You may want to flip to the section you feel applies to you on any certain day.

About half of the affirmations in this book are not separated into any category, as I feel these are the ones anyone can use effectively. They are under the Main/Miscellaneous section.

In whatever way you choose to experience this book, may I say thank you for allowing me into your consciousness, and I have faith in you and your continued success in your life journey.

Sharon Elaine

INTRODUCTION

Affirmations help us to consciously create. If we don't notice what we're saying to ourselves, we'll often not pick up on emotional signals within our bodies either. Both of these tools lay dormant while we flail around, thrashing from one disappointment to another, blaming others and making excuses as we go.

By reading this book, you have chosen to monitor your self-talk and make positive adjustments. You may find along the way that you begin to believe a bit differently about life. You may find yourself more positive and always expecting good things.

I urge you to not put any energy into trying to fake and pretend to be something you're not. Affirmation usage is not about covering up what you are thinking or believing, or pretending to act or be something you are not within this moment.

Affirmations are tools which allow you to focus your mind and your energies on that which you want to bring into creation. TRUTHS, if you will, that you have simply decided to not focus on for a time, and have allowed to wither around you.

Affirmations are tools that allow us to remain positively focused. When we don't consciously choose our words, or focus ourselves in a positive manner, we begin to feel lost and alone and feel there is no direction in life.

The steps below may be helpful when working on creating what you desire in life.

1.   Figure out what you want to experience… the life you want to live, and write it down if you wish.
2.   Be in a state of gratitude for all that you are and all that you have at this point in your life.

3.   Be in gratitude to yourself for having done your best, and release any resentment towards yourself (and others).

4.   Practice forgiveness with others, and most importantly, with yourself.

5.   Begin to form visions, feelings and self-talk that more closely match that which you wish to be experiencing in your life (in other words…day dream with feeling!)

6.   Start and continue a daily affirmation practice

7.   Focus on the positive within everything, and remain in joyful expectation of all the good you are now bringing into your life.

That's it. Don't make it a chore. No need to grudgingly say "I must do affirmations today, and if I don't I'm a bad person".

It is time for CONSCIOUS CREATING now, and you have taken a very powerful step in this process by allowing yourself to be open to affirmation usage.

It's only one tool in your toolbox, however, so remember to visualize and feel what you desire, and to expect them.   Don't wish for them. EXPECT THEM. You know something others do not… which is that you are creating quite a magnificent life for yourself, within yourself. They will find out soon enough, and when they begin to ask you how you did it, it will be fun to share this information with them.

It's up to you to change your life. It's up to you to take your negative self-talk and limiting beliefs and question them a bit. It's up to you to take responsibility for yourself, and make more positive, conscious choices.

IT IS UP TO YOU.

INSTRUCTIONAL CHAPTER

HOW TO USE AFFIRMATIONS:

There are different schools of thought on the exact method which works best for applying affirmations to your life. I will list the ones of which I'm aware, and you may try any that seem to suit your taste. I suggest trying each method until you find your preferences. You might start with the affirmation:
"<u>Affirmations work very well for me and in a short period of time</u>", which is the affirmation that helped me in the beginning.

WRITING-THEM-DOWN-METHOD:

Writing affirmations is widely-used. Many prefer this method, since it can be done with little or no discomfort, and is a reasonably quiet way to work. The quiet factor comes in handy when doing affirmations around other people (on public transportation, or on a work break, for instance).

With any affirmation use, the more repetitions, the better, as long as you are feeling positive emotions when using them. If the idea of doing 10 repetitions makes you cranky, don't do that many. Your energy vibration is always important, especially with affirmation use. A good rule of thumb is usually at least 3-10 per affirmation, per sitting. You may write each affirmation the complete 3-10 times, and then move onto the next one, or you may write different affirmations, one after the other, and then begin at the top of your list again.

TYPING-THEM-ON-A-COMPUTER METHOD:

This method is similar to the above method, but somewhat faster (assuming you can type faster than you can write). In this instance, I would recommend at least 20 repetitions of each affirmation (unless you're a very slow typist, in which case, stick with the 10).

I know of many people who type affirmations at work when they're feeling low. They spend a couple of minutes typing their favorite affirmations into a word processing computer program, clear their computer screen, then begin working on a new document.

When typing the affirmations for this book, I found myself more positive on a regular basis, so I know this technique works.

SAYING-THEM-ALOUD METHOD:

Another obvious tried-and-true method is the process of saying the affirmations out loud. This method is a bit more difficult when on public transportation, or in the grocery store or any place where lots of people would witness your self-talk. However, when in private, this is one of my favorite methods. I'll list here a few of the places and/or circumstances in which one might incorporate this technique.

1.   In your morning shower, or evening bath
2.   While blow-drying your hair (you have to speak up a bit, but it helps relieve the tedium of this chore)
3.   While washing dishes, or doing any general cleaning throughout the house

4.	In your car, no matter where you're going (this is a great trick for staying awake when driving on a long trip)
5.	Doing "mindless" exercises (like walking, or using stationary bicycles or treadmills)
6.	While getting dressed, shaving, putting on make-up or similar activities
7.	Any time you begin to feel negative energy

When saying affirmations aloud, keep a positive tone to your voice (without sounding fake, when at all possible). Repetition is required, just like any other method. However, the number of repetitions is not as important as the attitude when they are being said. Saying to yourself "I know I am a positive person" is fine. Saying this phrase 50 times between clinched teeth, rolling your eyes, giggling and guffawing would not be as effective as 10 said with belief, conviction and a positive tone to your voice.

DON'T LET MY ABOVE STATEMENT DETER YOU!!! If, in the beginning, you find yourself saying affirmations through clinched teeth, giggling, and so on, KEEP DOING THEM. These nervous habits will disappear as you become more confident.

SAYING-THEM-IN-YOUR-HEAD METHOD:

The main advantage of this method is being able to repeat the affirmations whenever you want and wherever you are. I know executives who begin thinking positive statements on their way to meetings, affirming that they will remain calm and loving and that the meeting will work out successfully for all involved.

Another advantage is that most of our thoughts are not spoken. Therefore, discovering and reversing negative thoughts will feel natural. When faced with confrontational situations, I often begin thinking affirmations before I choose the words I wish to speak.

SAYING-THEM-INTO-A-RECORDER,-THEN-LISTENING-TO-THEM METHOD:

Many of us like to listen to motivational tapes in our home, and especially in our automobile. Why not make your own? Recording the affirmations you've chosen, makes an ideal tape for use in driving to or from work, or on a stressful trip to any appointment that makes you feel nervous. (Examples: Visiting in-laws, doctor/dental visits, job interviews, etc.) It's also ideal to listen to this self-made tape when getting ready for work, as well as many of the already-mentioned activities. (Note: I also have a CD entitled "The Book of Affirmations (abridged)" which contains many spoken affirmations, available for purchase through my web site: www.unleashedminds.com)

Another advantage to this method is that others in the listening vicinity will benefit as well. When you choose to play a CD of affirmations, other passengers will have little choice but to listen along with you, and might remember helpful statements to use later. I know my three children have gained valuable insights from the types of CDs I choose to play in my vehicle. I'm now convinced that the words on these CDs are penetrating their consciousness, as evidenced by the positive statements I hear coming out of their mouths.

SAYING-THEM-INTO-A-MIRROR METHOD:

This is by far the most controversial method. Who amongst us hasn't been taught that staring at our reflection is vain? And I'm not just telling you to stare into a mirror, I'm telling you to talk to yourself at the same time. Potentially scary stuff, yes?   If you are instantly at ease with this method, great! If not, start with other methods, and continue this method until you feel ready for this one.

Start off this method by scanning your face as you begin your verbal affirmations. You may use internal or external speaking, while you look into your reflection. Continue until you're comfortable and then move on to looking directly into your eyes, as this heightens the effectiveness.

For anyone who looks in the mirror to comb hair, shave, put on make-up or brush teeth, this method can be used at those times, as well. By this time, you realize that repetitions are necessary, and you may choose any number that suits your needs.

Don't feel you have to limit yourself to only one or two of these methods. I use ALL of these methods, at various times of the day or week, depending on my mood, and circumstances. Experiment, have fun, and you'll see how quickly your life begins to change for the better.

The bottom line is, do whatever works best and is most comfortable for you. If what you're doing is uncomfortable or not enjoyable, chances are you won't stick with it (kind of like finding the activity you enjoy in order to stick with exercise). Therefore, it's imperative to keep searching until you find the affirmation method you feel matches your personality and needs.

It may appear this book contains conflicting statements of affirmation. Since I do not propose to be the ultimate authority on the workings of the mind and the Universe, I have joined together some conflicting viewpoints. All the affirmations are positive in nature. Your task is to choose the positive statements that work for you, within your own belief system.

You will find affirmations of many different lengths. Some seem meaty, deep and intense, while others seem like simplistic fluff. This is intentional. When arising, I find I'm more apt to use a light, simple statement, as the meaty ones seem too deep at 6:00 in the morning. In the evening, I like to think deep thoughts, so the longer ones are the ones I reach for. All lengths of affirmations are equal and helpful, use what appeals to you.

Thinking positively is not the ultimate goal of the user of affirmations. Realizing we have the option on how to react to situations, events and thoughts is a huge step on our path towards overall personal freedom. Monitoring and altering our self-talk remains a powerful tool in this process.

Mostly, I use affirmations to re-direct my internal chatter, and to obtain a peaceful, loving and joyful mind and life. My own personal belief is that "negative" and "positive" are necessary, as they are only perceptions and are all ultimately part of the Oneness. We create negative thoughts naturally and with little or no effort (for some inexplicable reason). Consciously choosing positive thoughts is a challenge I've accepted, and it has rewarded me enormously in personal growth. Conscious (vs. unconscious, old-programming) thinking is a challenge I recommend highly.

HOW TO GET STARTED:

Three affirmations I recommend using to help you begin your affirmation journey, are as follows: (Remember, you may use any of the above methods to incorporate these statements.)

1. Affirmations work very well for me in a very short period of time
2. I remember to say my affirmations at my appointed times
3. I catch negative thoughts and turn them into affirmations

Continue repeating these three statements until you feel comfortable, and wish to continue.

For the next few affirmations, I recommend using some that deal with self-love and forgiveness. There are many such statements throughout the book. At any time, you're encouraged to delve into the categories that are listed in the front of this book.

MAKING UP YOUR OWN AFFIRMATIONS:

Please begin to make up your own affirmations, at any time during the reading of this book. There is a never-ending supply of affirmation ideas, and mine may or may not coincide with your needs. The only rules to follow include: writing in a positive nature, writing in the present tense, and making them personal. Above all, have fun with them, and let your natural creative juices flow.

You may also feel free to use this book as a fortune cookie of sorts. Hold in your mind the thought or question, then flip open the book for an affirmation or two. I believe you'll find the ones that reveal themselves to you are just the ones you need.

Well, it's time to get started. You're off to a great start, on an incredible journey. You've taken the first step on the journey into the transformation of your thoughts, and therefore, into the transformation of your life.

Thank you again for allowing me into your consciousness. We are equal and intimately connected spirits along this life path and into eternity.

Much Success, Love and Joy!   Sharon Elaine

MAIN / MISCELLANEOUS

1 My heart and feelings belong to me
2 I am worthy
3 I deserve total freedom and prosperity
4 I attract all good things unto me
5 I deserve to fulfill my life purpose
6 I am fit and healthy
7 I perform very well on 6-8 hours of sleep a night
8 I deserve to be free from guilt
9 I deserve to be free from shame
10 I deserve to be free from fear
11 I deserve to BE
12 I deserve to discover who I am and why I'm here
13 I am worthy of all that is good and joyous
14 I deserve the best of everything
15 I deserve all the good that comes to me and through me
16 Giggling is good for me, so I giggle often
17 I am capable of doing all that I choose in this life
18 I am important
19 I am fulfilling my life's work
20 It's okay to pamper myself
21 I have faith in myself
22 I have faith in my abilities
23 I am a calm and stable influence to those around me
24 I discover more of my abilities every day
25 I am confident and try new things regularly
26 I am brave and calmly stand up for myself
27 I enjoy speaking my truth
28 I have power over my thoughts
29 It's okay when people disagree, I love them anyway
30 I like myself even when others act as if they don't
31 I make conscious choices
32 I am compassionate
33 As I prosper, everyone around me prospers
34 It's okay to prosper
35 I am confident in all I do
36 I am able to handle all that comes my way
37 My life is proceeding just right for my highest good

38 I welcome prosperity into all areas of my life
39 Things are now looking up
40 I deserve a peaceful life now and forever
41 I have a high opinion of myself
42 I choose to be a positive example in all I say and do
43 I am thankful for being alive
44 I get out of my own way
45 I enjoy all aspects of my life
46 I choose my destiny
47 I am a part of something wonderful
48 I am free of negative influences
49 Positive people are drawn to me
50 Fantasy is reality that hasn't happened yet
51 My feelings towards myself improve daily
52 I feel absolutely marvelous
53 It's all right to have a wonderful day when others don't
54 My life always has wonder and fulfillment
55 I always make the most of what I'm given
56 My good opinion of myself remains constant
57 I retain a healthy attitude through adversity
58 I need answer only to myself
59 I deserve to be who I am
60 I deserve to be powerful
61 It's okay to be proud of who I am
62 It's okay to be proud of what I've accomplished
63 I hold my own opinion, even if it differs from others
64 I feel completely calm
65 I see the big picture of my life
66 I am rich in all things and in every area of my life
67 I give thanks for my existence
68 I am in charge of what I think
69 I like being who I am
70 I remain healthy physically, mentally and emotionally
71 Life is filled with fun and excitement
72 Tears are a part of me, and it's okay to shed them
73 I'm as good and important as anyone else
74 My desires are good and part of what makes me who I am
75 All that I do is for good
76 I laugh easily and often
77 It's okay to be fine

78 It's okay to be fantastic
79 It's okay to make outrageous plans for my future
80 Taking time for me is acceptable to me today
81 I understand more about myself every day
82 My needs are easily met
83 Every day I discover new things that interest me
84 Every day I cultivate new interests
85 Luxurious living is something I deserve
86 My thoughts and feelings are my friends
87 I live every moment to its fullest
88 Time waits for me
89 Time is my friend
90 Living is a joyous experience
91 I consciously remain focused
92 I experiment with new and different activities
93 All of my questions are answered in their own time
94 Wonderful events take place in my life daily
95 I now believe everything will turn out all right
96 Willingness to accept my freedom is now mine
97 I am now judgment-free
98 I own all of my emotions
99 I'm learning to accept all of who I am
100 My emotions are all good
101 Freedom is a concept I'm now willing to accept for myself
102 My mental capacities increase daily
103 Breathing deeply is something I remember to do often
104 I attain all the fame and recognition I wish to attain
105 I feel fabulous, now, in this moment
106 I am entitled to have my own opinion at all times
107 I treat others as I wish to be treated
108 I congratulate myself daily for my accomplishments
109 It's okay to have the spotlight directed at me
110 My accomplishments deserve to be noticed
111 I set my own pace
112 My life is a string of wonderful events
113 I'm smart enough for all that I choose to do
114 People are captivated by my personality and charm
115 I'm impressive to myself
116 I can make a name for myself if I choose
117 I have a healthy lifestyle

118 I hold a positive mental outlook
119 Tenderness is one of my attributes
120 I choose to ignore insults or putdowns
121 I am calm when put in the limelight
122 It's easy for me to say hello to everyone I see
123 Smiling at others helps me, as well as them
124 I'm a good sport
125 I'm having a wonderful time
126 My life is worry-free
127 I have a great sense of humor
128 Sometimes I feel a little nutty and that's okay
129 Experiencing life makes me smile
130 I feel sensational
131 I go with the flow of life
132 My conscious tears help to cleanse my soul
133 I'm going to make it
134 I choose my life's adventures
135 I stitch the pattern of my life together beautifully
136 I am who I want to be
137 I teach others and others teach me
138 I perceive freedom and opportunity everywhere
139 I believe we are all created equal
140 My heart is full of compassion
141 I have an abundance of gifts to share with the world
142 My confidence is an attribute
143 Having confidence comes naturally to me
144 I am an important investment
145 I am outgoing and free from shyness
146 I trust my gut feelings
147 Life is one fun activity after another
148 I treat myself the way I'd like others to treat me
149 I treat myself very well
150 I accept my housing as a safe haven
151 I jump into the game of life
152 I am free from prejudices
153 I relax into the rhythm of my life
154 I recognize and embrace all emotions
155 I am free from illusions
156 I am the master over my time
157 I deserve total freedom

158 I take good care of myself
159 I know what I want out of life
160 It's okay to make my own decisions
161 I am affected by only positive energy
162 Anything and everything is possible
163 It's natural for me to treat others well
164 I'm okay all the time, in every circumstance
165 I embrace any challenges and changes
166 I am now free from jealousy
167 I'm as important as my favorite celebrity
168 Expressing gratitude comes naturally to me
169 I communicate well at all times
170 My communication skills improve daily
171 I set my imagination free
172 Today I give myself a break
173 I'm as good as anyone else
174 I retain my good mood through all things
175 Overcoming obstacles is easy for me
176 My mind responds well to mental exercises
177 Thinking I look good is okay
178 It's all right to feel comfortable with my looks
179 I'm able to ignore any negative influences
180 I enjoy being nice to strangers
181 Sexy is a good word to describe me
182 Intelligent is a good word to describe me
183 Confident is a good word to describe me
184 I deserve to be around positive, interesting people
185 I expect good things to happen, and they do
186 I expect my life to change in a positive way, and it does
187 All the choices I make are good ones
188 The choices I make are appropriate for me
189 I am able to think clearly in all circumstances
190 I move with beauty and grace
191 I'm relaxed in all situations
192 I take people's advice and do with it what I choose
193 Beauty is around me at all times
194 It's okay that I'm an independent spirit
195 I remain alert when I need to be
196 I am alert now, in this moment
197 I'm more powerful every day

198 I believe in myself and I show that to the world today
199 I have high ideals and I stick to them
200 Today I take advantage of being alive
201 Today I use my talents to their utmost
202 I deserve a new, beautiful vehicle that I easily afford
203 My life gets better and better every day
204 I'm able to retain my unique sense of style at all times
205 Every day I find out more about who I am
206 Discovering who I am is very exciting and fun
207 Everything always works out for the best
208 I am calm and confident always
209 My muscles relax with every breath
210 It's okay to continue to feel wonderful
211 It's okay to continue to prosper
212 It's okay to hold a positive attitude even when others don't
213 I deserve lots of positive experiences
214 My mind is relaxed and receptive to guidance
215 Releasing my past is a wise choice
216 I'm beautiful inside and out
217 I create my own solutions to my life challenges
218 While showering, I see my worries flowing down the drain
219 I have an overall upbeat attitude about life
220 I remember to breathe deeply on a regular basis
221 I am guilt-free and loving it
222 I am free to be anything I choose
223 I am free to act any way I choose
224 I am dedicated to the task at hand
225 I enjoy my environment
226 I belong
227 I'm tremendously important
228 I feel things deeply and that's okay
229 Knowing I can, I choose to keep my spirits up
230 I accept responsibility over my actions
231 I'm excited about my life
232 I live in the moment
233 I let God take care of the Universe
234 I accept a harmonious lifestyle
235 I am brilliant
236 The best in me is yet to come
237 I'm perfect right now, in this moment

238 I choose to live my destiny
239 I choose to keep up my enthusiasm for life
240 I choose to feel worthwhile
241 I deserve to feel worthwhile
242 I remain calm while planning my future
243 I am free from all forms of jealousy
244 I am free from all forms of anger
245 It's easy to imagine myself where I want to be
246 Everyone I meet with today is kind and loving
247 I calmly bless all that is around me
248 I calmly bless all that is within me
249 Today I remember that every moment is a miracle
250 I relax into my future
251 I choose to let insults roll off my back today
252 It's okay to live by my own ideals
253 I choose to be relaxed and content
254 I deserve to have a really great mail day
255 Affirmations really work
256 My happiness is permanent
257 I deserve to live a charmed existence
258 My tastes are simple; I choose the best of everything
259 I value my own opinion
260 I can concentrate on one thing at a time if I choose
261 I can concentrate on many things at once if I choose
262 All people are inherently good
263 You and I are equal
264 I believe in total equality
265 My mind is clear and I'm good at making decisions
266 I do deep breathing regularly to get the jitters out
267 Communicating with myself is something I do well
268 I appreciate who I am and what I can do
269 My self-worth runs high
270 I retain my good sense of humor through all things
271 I am calm in all circumstances
272 I keep my hopes set high
273 I am who I choose to be
274 I've conquered any problems with authority figures
275 I relax into the flow of my life
276 I am released from feelings of inadequacy
277 I focus well on all projects

278 I have found my niche in the world
279 It's time for amazing people like me to step forward
280 I'm very talented
281 I have an extraordinary sense of style
282 I choose to let go of any antagonistic feelings
283 I have great role models
284 I am free from labels
285 I am free from comparisons
286 I choose whom I wish to emulate
287 I believe in what I'm doing
288 I believe in myself
289 Positive thoughts are what I enjoy most
290 I have as much promise as everyone else
291 I have as much to offer the world as anyone
292 My mind is a powerful tool
293 I have the perfect vehicle for my needs
294 I am what I want to be
295 I deserve to be surrounded by beautiful things
296 I always look on the positive side of everything
297 Absolutely anything is possible
298 I deserve to be surrounded by positive people
299 I know my goals and I'm working to fulfill them
300 I respond very well to good treatment
301 I'm starting off on the right foot today
302 Today I remember to think before I act
303 Every way I look at things we all win
304 I choose to be unaffected by negative thoughts
305 I choose actions that are therapeutic today
306 I choose thoughts that are therapeutic today
307 I deserve to ride in limousines regularly
308 I remain rational at all times
309 I am my own best friend
310 I'm here to find the best that can happen today
311 I'm here to have some fun today
312 I can do anything I put my mind to
313 I spend my time wisely today
314 Delegating authority is easy for me
315 It's okay for my life to be easy
316 It's okay for my life to run smoothly
317 I am secure in myself and my abilities

318 I remain excited about my possibilities
319 I choose to remain focused during good times
320 I express myself clearly at all times
321 I am highly creative
322 I find it easy to apologize when I want to
323 My anger is a part of me I can accept
324 I choose to be anger-free
325 I choose to be in touch with my feelings
326 I'm able to alter the course of my life
327 I let only positive thoughts enter my consciousness
328 I'm free from unneeded hunger
329 I accept only positive outcomes
330 I am as I choose to be
331 I behave as I choose to behave
332 Keeping my spirits up is easy for me
333 My living arrangements suit me perfectly
334 I need only me to make myself feel important
335 It's okay to be who I am
336 I'm deeply grateful for my existence
337 I choose how to respond to events in my life
338 I choose to admire myself
339 I expect and accept wonderful surprises from the Universe
340 Today I'm on the look out for all things good
341 The love I have for myself grows each day
342 With each breath, I visualize health and well-being
343 I am saturated with powerful golden white healing light
344 My body thanks me for the positive focus I have with it now
345 My body and Self are becoming closer, faithful friends
346 I allow the Universe to shower help upon me today
347 My energy systems are now clear and flow freely
348 Clear, healing energy flushes through my organs and cells
349 I love me, all of me, all the time
350 I choose health
351 I now have more energy than ever before
352 I'm quickly finishing projects and feeling joyful doing it
353 I spend time in solitude today to refresh my entire being
354 I release any thoughts of worry or doubt
355 I am now firmly focused within faith and joyful expectation
356 My life keeps getting better and better every moment
357 I remain calm and happy all day today

358 I allow myself to claim more joy and abundance now
359 Now, in this moment, I am healthy, wealthy and joyful
360 I relax and allow the Universe to guide me today
361 I treat my body well today, and it thanks me for it
362 It's easy for me to complete projects, so I do so today
363 This moment I become more joyful, centered and balanced
364 I take deep breaths of joy today
365 I let richness shower over me
366 It's time for me to become all that I desire to become
367 I relax my body completely and let the energy flow
368 I take a few moments today to breathe in love
369 I take a few moments today to breathe love out to others
370 I find joy in completing my projects today
371 I send love out to the world
372 The world responds with love to me
373 My body is healing itself quickly and easily
374 I love me, all of me, all the time
375 I now take time to notice what I do, say, feel and believe
376 I am the most important focus of my day today
377 I help others by learning to know myself
378 I take this moment and go further inward
379 I have great spirits who help me on my internal path
380 I throw old ideas and beliefs out the window and start anew
381 Taking deep breaths helps me connect with my inner self
382 I have the time to go inward today
383 I have plenty of time to go inward for decisions
384 I stay alert today
385 I notice what I am thinking, feeling and believing
386 I allow clarity into what I am now choosing to create
387 I am now able to quickly change what I create
388 I feel positive energy as I make conscious choices
389 I dramatically alter my life right now, in this moment
390 I now remember that truly anything is possible
391 I give myself time to visualize and FEEL my new creations
392 With every breath I have more and more energy today
393 I allow myself to completely relax today
394 My work will wait, it's important for me to relax now
395 I take deep, conscious breaths and feel the energy flowing
396 I focus on my breath and thank it for keeping me alive
397 I thank my body for all the work it does for me every day

398 I send gratitude to all my organs and cells
399 I breathe the colors of healing into my cells
400 I breathe healing into my aura and into the Universe
401 I am the most important person in my life
402 Today I choose to focus on nurturing my body
403 Today I choose to let the Universe nurture my entire being
404 I allow others to help me today
405 I allow the Universe to help me today
406 I am so grateful for all that I have created
407 I am grateful to the Universe for help with my creations
408 I continue to do affirmations to help me in my creations
409 I stay positive about life and always find the good
410 I have more blessings than I can count
411 I banish all negative thoughts from my consciousness
412 I shake all negative thoughts out of my system
413 I am more confident today than yesterday
414 For now, I set aside negative thoughts
415 Every day offers unlimited potential
416 The interesting and exciting part of life has now begun
417 I'm a nice person
418 I have a lot going for me
419 I have good ideas
420 I deserve to go everywhere first class
421 I am free of all jealousy
422 I believe the sky's the limit
423 Time works for me
424 I have abilities to branch out in all directions
425 The world now beats a path to my door
426 I'm free of fear of success
427 Feeling sorry for myself is now a part of my past
428 I have room in my life for all good things
429 I easily take care of myself
430 Trusting my hunches and gut feelings works for me
431 Nurturing others comes naturally to me
432 Nurturing myself comes naturally to me
433 My life is right on track
434 I give myself permission to be prosperous
435 Relaxation is good and easy for me
436 I stay in touch with long-distance friends and relatives
437 I give my heart away, and receive it back

438 I take time to catch my breath daily
439 I'm doing just fine
440 I'm ready to get my show on the road
441 I choose to live
442 People like me better when I like myself
443 I am as good as everyone else
444 My ideas have merit
445 My ideas are as good as anyone else's
446 I deserve to leave my worries behind
447 Water is refreshing; I drink 8 glasses a day
448 I am continually in a state of grace
449 It's possible to be excited and calm at the same time
450 I'm here for the ride and my view is great
451 I respect myself
452 I evaluate each decision and make good choices
453 Loving thinking comes easily to me
454 I feel very secure within myself
455 I have the intelligence to do anything I choose
456 I'm secure within all of my relationships
457 I choose to taste the world in which I live today
458 It's okay to make decisions based on my gut feelings
459 My life has many more ups than downs
460 I am a peaceful being
461 I exist and I am loved
462 I am a good person, no matter what
463 I relax and receive guidance
464 Fresh air heals me, so I breathe deeply today
465 I remember to communicate with nature daily
466 I'm an inspiration to myself and others
467 My moods are a part of me
468 Being what some people call moody, is okay
469 I'm incredibly thankful today
470 In my life's journey I've got a window seat
471 I'm thrilled with what I've accomplished in my life so far
472 Destiny is calling and I feel myself answering
473 My life proceeds wonderfully well at all times
474 Great opportunities fall into my lap today
475 I'm thankful with every breath I take
476 I'm high quality
477 I remember everyone I meet has their own challenges

478 My personality suits me
479 My personality is colorful and interesting
480 I allow my abundance to arrive
481 I release all doubts from my being
482 I listen very well
483 I'm a wonderful listener
484 I allow others to have different points of view
485 I relinquish the activity of arguing
486 I choose all activities in my life wisely
487 Today I choose to find people to admire
488 I release all nervous feelings from my being
489 My ship comes in today
490 I am an expert at working with affirmations
491 I deserve to take really good care of myself
492 When I speak my mind, it clears my head
493 It's okay to receive compliments
494 I now release all butterflies from my stomach
495 Destiny is calling and I answer now, in this moment
496 Today I share my talents and skills with humanity
497 Today I learn something from everyone I meet
498 I gain knowledge from many different sources today
499 I easily find my way in life
500 I have a great sense of direction
501 Getting lost is in my past and I release it now
502 My self-worth is determined by me
503 My life always has meaning
504 I feel very confident today
505 I give and receive praise today
506 I notice only the good in people today
507 I think I look just fine
508 There are many ways to feel wealthy; I discover them all
509 Life has dealt me a wonderful hand and I'm playing it well
510 I remain constant in my positive beliefs
511 I'm willing to entertain the possibility of change
512 I accept the generosity of others today
513 My destiny is my own
514 I claim my destiny
515 I claim my prosperity
516 I have decided to be prosperous
517 I am free from discouragement

518 I am in demand
519 I feel good about myself regardless of my actions
520 My life is carefree
521 I am courageous and loving
522 I approve of myself
523 I possess an excellent memory
524 I let go of all frustrations today
525 I have the support of everyone around me
526 I'm easily able to focus on any activity I choose
527 I ask all the right questions today
528 Today I choose to listen really carefully
529 I articulate my thoughts very well
530 It's okay to let someone else be the life of the party
531 Things can only get better
532 I'm clever and creative in all I say and do
533 I have very good ideas
534 It's okay to be excited about my accomplishments
535 I dedicate my life to the causes I see fit
536 It's okay to want more
537 It's okay to want to have it all
538 My fondest wishes have been granted
539 I give myself lots of treats today
540 It's okay to baby myself
541 Whatever happens, I keep my faith
542 There is a great goodness in humanity
543 I trust myself again
544 I treat myself like royalty today
545 I always explain my views clearly and calmly
546 I listen to the desires of my heart
547 I think things through and have lots of time to decide
548 I'm proud to be hanging in there
549 I give myself credit for all the kindness I extend
550 I can be whatever I need to be at any given moment
551 I can do whatever I need to do in any given moment
552 It's easy for me to ignore all rumors
553 My feelings are tremendously important
554 I handle all pressures with style and grace
555 It's okay to feel my sorrow
556 I focus on my power to transform my life
557 I concentrate on my abilities today

558 People listen when I express my opinions
559 I'm free from the negative opinions of others
560 All my wishes are coming true
561 All of my emotions are necessary for my existence
562 I choose today to unmask a new me
563 Today I reveal to the world who I truly am
564 There are many more things in life to discover
565 I'm able to shrug off potentially distressing news
566 Daily I make plans and happily complete them
567 Opportunities are all around me
568 I'm an individual and I address my individual needs
569 I meet all the people I admire within my lifetime
570 I leave all suspicious actions in my past
571 It's okay to ask a lot of questions
572 I take command of my life
573 I easily resolve any potential conflicts
574 Anything worth getting is worth getting quickly
575 I let other people solve their own problems
576 I release my attachment to solving others' problems
577 I deserve to have massages on a regular basis
578 I stay aware of possibilities today and always
579 Seeing others as myself helps me to understand them
580 I treat all animals with respect
581 Animals and I get along very well
582 Today I discover my purpose in life
583 I choose to have fun in every moment
584 I choose only mentally healthy shows to watch on TV
585 I remember to notice the beauty in all things today
586 Every day I understand myself more
587 I release all negative and I now accept all positive
588 All purchases I make are correct for me
589 I truly like people and they like me
590 I'm a people-person
591 I am now free of bad breath
592 I remember to follow the hygiene habits I've chosen
593 Brushing my teeth twice a day is a habit for me
594 I'm open to suggestions from all positive sources
595 Conflicts I have with others are easily resolved today
596 I am free of conflicts today
597 I choose to have all conflicts resolved today

598 I'm very satisfied with the way my life is turning out
599 Even when I'm tired, I think clearly
600 I am secure within myself and my abilities
601 Today I connect with everything and everyone around me
602 I love the town in which live
603 The town I live in loves me
604 I am rich beyond measure
605 I am friends with all police officers
606 I always find the lowest prices when I shop
607 I am part of a good and kind Universe
608 On the journey of life, I'm given all that I need
609 I'm far wealthier than I realize
610 I am free of the need to control other people's lives
611 I am easily able to spot a con
612 I always assume everyone is doing his or her best
613 It's easy to give people the benefit of the doubt
614 I always take time to think before I speak
615 Today I let the other person finish speaking before I speak
616 I receive guidance daily from a higher power
617 I relax every fiber of my being
618 I focus on the good in every situation
619 I pass down through the generations only the values I wish
620 I am free to hold my own values
621 I now free myself from my past
622 The truth is always all right to speak
623 How I choose to perceive others' comments is up to me
624 My opinion of myself is the one that truly matters
625 I'm much calmer now, in this moment
626 I now feel calmness washing over me
627 I believe in remaining calm in all situations
628 When it all comes down to it, it's all up to me
629 I always want what's best for me
630 I am free of gossip
631 Only I know what's truly best for me
632 I spend my time constructively
633 I'm always mentally prepared for everything
634 I'm always emotionally prepared for everything
635 Insults bounce off of me and leave me unaffected
636 My emotional temperature is always at love
637 I am free of the role of victim

638 With every new experience I gain vast knowledge
639 I make a conscious effort to learn from everything in life
640 Whatever happens, I'm gonna be okay
641 What is right for my life is determined by me
642 My life, and all life, is precious
643 The answers to all my questions are stored within me
644 I put all anger aside today
645 Any feelings of betrayal I release now
646 My memory is a part of me and is always reliable
647 Everything I do, I do with love
648 There's plenty of time to get done what needs to be done
649 I go with my gut feelings 100% of the time
650 I know exactly what I want
651 I know myself better than anyone else does
652 I've transcended boredom
653 The hysteria in my life is settling down now
654 Everyone respects my privacy
655 I'm now free of superficiality
656 I'm figuring out what means the most to me
657 I'm free from believing in body odor
658 Every one of my acts is an unselfish act
659 Every action I take is for my good and the good of others
660 There's always a chance for goodness to take over
661 Today I set my tortured mind free
662 I have the skills it takes to master my life challenges
663 I'm okay as I am and I choose to get even better
664 I'm now free of any desire to whine
665 I'm now free from speaking untruths
666 My vehicle and I are forming a positive relationship
667 My appliances and I are forming a positive relationship
668 I always behave at peak performance
669 Terrific people continually come into my life
670 Discovering my true potential is rewarding
671 I learn grand lessons today
672 Telling others what to do is part of my past and I let it go
673 I like the way I walk
674 I like the way I talk
675 I'm free of procrastinating
676 There is always time to listen to the other point of view
677 My thoughts are powerful, and I choose them wisely

678 The words I use today are always positive and supportive
679 I'm productive when I put my mind and heart to any task
680 My vehicle always runs in perfect condition
681 I'm finished with feeling sorry for myself
682 I choose to understand all sides of an issue
683 I now visualize my life exactly as I wish it to be
684 I remember to visualize my life in the positive
685 I choose to visualize my day going smoothly in all areas
686 Visualization is easy for me
687 Today I reach my full potential
688 Today I visualize finishing all I set my mind to
689 I am viewed by others as a positive person
690 I view myself as a positive person
691 I now completely trust my hair stylist
692 My disposition is always one of which I can be proud
693 I trust and listen to my hunches
694 I'm connected with my personal power
695 It's comfortable for me to change for the better
696 I find the correct people to assist me on my path
697 I deserve the best and I get what I want
698 I pay attention to all the things I want and retain that focus
699 I consciously choose to relax
700 Terrific opportunities come my way today
701 I'm free from worrying over things that haven't happened
702 I direct my attention to the positive side of life
703 I help humanity by helping myself
704 Every day I become more responsible
705 Every day I become more joyful and playful
706 Everything has a positive side
707 I always have exquisite manners
708 I make time for fun today
709 I'm always able to stay out of trouble
710 All is going well in my life
711 I easily overcome any dark thoughts
712 I'm vibrant and alive
713 Everything happens in its own time
714 Every day I discover more of what makes me unique
715 I'm becoming a better reader every day
716 I'm always happy with the decisions I make
717 I retain information from everything I read

718 My choice of reading material is improving daily
719 I'd rather read a good book than watch television
720 Today I read something filled with insights for me
721 Everything I choose to read, brings me many insights
722 I've chosen to relinquish anger and the pain it causes
723 When it comes to clothing, I'm developing my own style
724 I remember to take my daily vitamins
725 I like the sound of my voice
726 I have the freedom and confidence to be myself
727 I learn from any and all mistakes
728 It's okay to sing out loud in the car
729 I'm always around whenever I need me
730 I know everything always works out all right
731 I have a great and kind sense of humor
732 It's okay to be spontaneous
733 I'm calm and centered, now and always
734 I believe it when people say I'm beautiful
735 In the winter I always stay warm
736 In the summer I always stay cool
737 I'm as good a person as all the people on television
738 It's okay to just be quiet
739 Today I rest my troubled mind
740 I allow myself to prosper today
741 I've survived much in this life and I continue to survive
742 I'm becoming better looking every day
743 Insights come to me from many different sources
744 Every choice I make is the right one
745 I expect great things to happen today, so they do
746 I completely relax into the moment
747 I'm very knowledgeable when it comes to car buying
748 I'm knowledgeable when it comes to repairing my vehicle
749 I remember to get my car tuned-up at its scheduled times
750 I'm happy I know how to operate my vehicle effectively
751 I always drive with caution and a pinch of patience
752 A positive attitude is the most important accessory I wear
753 I always easily affirm myself out of a dark mood
754 I enjoy every aspect of my life
755 I perform all my daily functions well
756 What matters is that I like myself
757 I excuse others for insensitive behavior

758 I get along better with kids every day
759 I have my wits about me today
760 I always have the ability to rally back and win
761 I always extend myself in a loving and open manner
762 Tender words are always welcomed
763 I'm very good at relaxing on cue
764 In this moment I choose to be free
765 I like my laugh
766 Freedom is a concept I'm now accepting
767 I enjoy and appreciate art and artists
768 My temper is always under control
769 I overcome all obstacles today
770 I have all the skills I need to perform well in life
771 It's easy for me to say I'm sorry
772 Remembering to write letters is easier for me now
773 I accept apologies easier each time
774 I always pay my bills on time, with money left over
775 It's okay to act differently than those around me
776 I choose to be free from sticking my foot in my mouth
777 How I respond to my life is my choice
778 I am able to stay alert through all I do today
779 I choose to have many "days in the sun"
780 It's okay to have excitement in my belly
781 I release all my insecurities
782 In the end, the decision is always mine
783 Ultimately I make all decisions in my life
784 It's logical to visualize great outcomes
785 When angry, I practice relaxation techniques
786 My accomplishments are many
787 I am free of competition
788 I fit my unique piece into the world's puzzle
789 I'm an exquisite creation with zero defects
790 How I handle conflict is up to me
791 The time is now for change
792 I'm ecstatic about my life possibilities
793 I give up the attraction to behaving badly
794 I now put my plans into action
795 I remain positive and calm today
796 I accept only positive comments about myself and others
797 I'm completely satisfied in this moment

798 I am free from all restrictions
799 What everyone else does and what I do can be different
800 I have the ability to change my life in an instant
801 It's okay for me to be the one to instigate a conversation
802 I live my life by listening to my instincts
803 The words "ought" and "should" are out of my vocabulary
804 I release archaic thoughts and ideas
805 Being content with my life is all right
806 There is more to life than me
807 It enriches me when I compliment others
808 Today I choose to write a thank-you note or two
809 I use all of my time constructively
810 I smile at everyone with whom I make contact today
811 My positive attitude is contagious
812 I am thankful down to every cell of my body
813 I always have control over my actions
814 I'm finished with feeling sorry for myself
815 I respect other people's privacy
816 I'm free from the desire to lose my temper
817 I feel like a million bucks
818 I enjoy cleaning the house
819 I like doing the laundry
820 I always have help when I choose to clean the house
821 Everyone sees how kind and understanding I am
822 I listen to my heart and follow its instructions
823 It's okay to release anger from this situation
824 I'm mature enough to handle all of my responsibilities
825 Giving myself a pat on the back is very good
826 Giving someone else a pat on the back is very good
827 I always give credit where credit is due
828 I thank people appropriately today
829 I remember to thank everyone in my life often
830 I find it comfortable to hug others
831 I choose to give away hugs to everyone in my life
832 I enjoy giving and receiving hugs and do it often
833 I'm a thoughtful person and think of others' feelings
834 I choose to share my experience with the world today
835 I make a difference today
836 Today I refuse to spread lies
837 I've decided to give up gossiping now

838 I deserve fresh flowers regularly
839 I'm responsible for all of my actions
840 I'm responsible for how I act and react in any situation
841 People are really all the same
842 I'm as important and necessary as anyone else
843 I'm as deserving as anyone else
844 Today I ask people how they feel and I really listen
845 I'm mentally able to relax and take it easy today
846 I'm physically able to relax and take it easy today
847 I allow myself the luxuries of life
848 When the telephone rings, I expect and get good news
849 There's always room for creativity in any project
850 I'm on time for everything I do today
851 I give myself permission to be calm
852 I always have a calm disposition
853 Curiosity is a part of me and helps me learn
854 I share what I have and know with others
855 It's okay when things are going easily and well
856 I'm known as a person who gets things done
857 I win the support of influential people and organizations
858 It's okay to have a lot on my mind; I can still relax
859 I'm emotional and sensitive and that's a good thing
860 I take all comments toward me as compliments
861 I enjoy challenging situations
862 It's okay to enjoy the kindness of strangers
863 I notice all goodness around me
864 I have countless blessings in all areas of my life
865 I have my own personal style and I love it
866 The people that I care about, care about me
867 My future looks amazingly bright
868 There are many places I want to visit, and I know I will
869 I'm a grown-up and I act like it… when I want to
870 There are things worth standing up for
871 I feel like my life is changing for the better daily
872 When I increase my self worth, the sky's the limit
873 Daily I prove to myself that I deserve the best
874 I hold onto my convictions
875 I have a firm grasp on my present and future
876 I remember my past fondly, and with healing energy
877 Every detail of my life suits me perfectly

878 I take good care of myself
879 I make big decisions easily and quickly
880 I'm known as someone who can make it happen
881 Rest and relaxation is good for my mind, body and soul
882 I'm around the people who do me the most good
883 When I want to be left alone, I am
884 When I want company, I attract positive, loving company
885 Complaining is part of my past and I now let it go
886 I'm my own person 100% of the time
887 When I choose to be, I'm very persuasive
888 It's okay to get something off my chest
889 I own my depression and I can choose to release it
890 I'm alive, I'm a survivor
891 I'm taking my life back now
892 The position I hold in life is up to me
893 I've decided to refrain from cheating
894 Today I get my act into gear
895 It's okay to go places alone
896 Circumstances are always within my control
897 I always discuss issues calmly
898 Tortured thoughts are in my past and I release them
899 My feelings of helplessness are gone
900 I'm excited to see the outcome of my positive actions
901 My fantasies become reality today
902 Selfishness is part of my past and I release it now
903 I'm free from underestimating my tomorrows
904 It's okay to cry and laugh whenever I choose
905 I'm now choose to cry less frequently
906 Deep breathing now takes the place of tears
907 My heart soars with the clouds today
908 I treat myself to spa treatments regularly
909 My qualifications as a positive human are excellent
910 I'm pleased with my appearance today and every day
911 Decisions that shape my life are best made by me
912 The direct communication approach works well for me
913 The time has come for me to live life fully
914 Grand ideas come into my consciousness today
915 It's okay to think big
916 I make all the right choices today
917 I choose to be carefree right now

918 I understand my emotions more each day
919 I'm getting in touch with my true emotions
920 I have what it takes to make it big
921 It's okay to have people count on me
922 I find it easy to catch my breath
923 I possess a never-ending supply of hope
924 I'm very talented in many areas of my life
925 I hold myself in high regard
926 I choose to completely relax now, in this moment
927 I remember to be fascinated with life
928 I clean up my act today
929 I'm finally able to realize my self-worth today
930 It's okay to feel that I'm a genius
931 I spend time today pleasing myself
932 I feel very free today
933 I demand the best of myself, and I always deliver
934 It's okay to have fun with life
935 I'm a multi-faceted individual
936 I'm good at a lot of different things
937 It's okay to act silly when I feel like it
938 It's okay to be what others would term as abnormal
939 I'm consistently winning contests and sweepstakes
940 I have the capacity for positive change
941 I have the ability to change my life for the better
942 I'm famous just as I am now
943 I'm important just as I am now
944 People find me fascinating today
945 I find myself fascinating today
946 I find others fascinating today
947 Fantastic events happen to me today
948 It's okay to feel I'm important
949 Today my high energy remains constant
950 I get good ideas from many interesting sources
951 I enjoy planning ahead
952 I remember to vote
953 It's okay to appear silly and be laughed at sometimes
954 I handle conflicts very well
955 I deserve the goodness I've been given
956 It's okay to feel nervous, and it's okay to feel calm
957 I can choose calmness at any time

958 I'm always where I need to be
959 I think on my feet
960 I see things in others that I recognize within myself
961 I'm able to make people understand what I'm feeling
962 I believe my life continues to get better
963 I'm enjoying myself more each day
964 My problems are diminishing rapidly
965 I attract people to me by being calm and loving
966 It's now easier talking to others about my problems
967 I'm always in the right place at the right time
968 I'm free from ever being involved in traffic accidents
969 I'm now free from feelings of worthlessness
970 I have the skills and the ability to do whatever I wish
971 I'm comfortable in everything I wear
972 I'm comfortable when I wear nothing
973 I walk and talk with confidence and grace
974 I'm now free to be totally myself in all situations
975 In the grand scheme of things, I matter
976 I work through what's making me feel sad
977 It's easier for me to define and embrace my feelings
978 I'm now able to release any old hurt feelings
979 I let go of any feelings of shame
980 I now throw guilt right out the window
981 I'm very in tune to the feelings and needs of others
982 I'm able to spend plenty of time with those I love
983 I easily decide what deals are right for me today
984 When purchasing a vehicle, I always make the right choice
985 All salespeople treat me with respect and love
986 I'm very knowledgeable when it comes to car buying
987 I'm finished with feeling unworthy
988 I'm now releasing any and all stubborn tendencies
989 I have a long, beautiful life ahead of me
990 Today I let my life happen smoothly
991 I know what I want and I allow it to come to me
992 It's okay to believe in fairy tales
993 I've given up judging myself and others
994 I'm now free from getting stuck in traffic jams
995 I ignore the harsh comments of others
996 I choose to dismiss doom and gloom messages
997 Today I believe I'm very sexy

998 I stand on my own two feet and face my challenges
999 I can be excited and calm at the same time
1000 I remember there are many ways of looking at things
1001 Today I give people a little slack
1002 Today I ignore the condescending remarks of others
1003 Today I enjoy the supportive remarks of others
1004 I choose to keep all the promises that I make
1005 When someone confides in me, I respect their privacy
1006 I take responsibility over my life
1007 I feel relaxed and refreshed today
1008 All life experiences are equal and wonderful
1009 I've decided to live fully today
1010 Times change rapidly and I choose to keep up
1011 I'm adventurous and attract other adventurous people
1012 I'm committed to bringing my visions into reality
1013 I send my life issues lots of love today
1014 I'm free from having to take care of the world
1015 The world is free to make up its own mind
1016 I'm free to make up my own mind
1017 What other people think of me is their choice
1018 I'm unaffected by what others think of me
1019 I now shed my need for approval
1020 It's okay to know what I want to be when I grow up
1021 It's okay to not know what I want to be when I grow up
1022 It's okay to always feel young inside
1023 I'm free from the view others have of me
1024 I only care what view I hold of myself
1025 I make the world a better place
1026 I choose to keep the day bright
1027 I have extraordinary gifts and lead an extraordinary life
1028 I embrace my own freedom
1029 I get many second winds throughout my day
1030 I can be humble and wondrous at the same time
1031 I'm now a grown-up and I love it
1032 I love the way my mind works
1033 I'm now free from holding grudges
1034 I can always go further than others think I can go
1035 I give my discouragement up for lent
1036 I'm okay, through and through
1037 Getting what I want is a trick I've mastered

1038 It's okay to digest new ideas and concepts daily
1039 I know affirmations work
1040 I'm free from wallowing in self-pity
1041 Having a wild streak inside me is okay
1042 I feel myself being pulled toward my destiny
1043 It's okay to be the star of my life
1044 All my problems are already solved
1045 I'm free from being upset with myself
1046 In my existence all is well
1047 It's okay to enjoy culinary delicacies regularly
1048 Today I take my own advice
1049 It's time I accept all the good that's coming to me
1050 I bounce back from troubles quickly now
1051 I always have a choice of how I want to react
1052 I ignore the flaws of others
1053 I have the ability to do many things at once
1054 It's okay to enjoy many types of entertainment
1055 I have something to believe in
1056 I'm exceptionally well-liked and respected
1057 I have so much I now choose to give
1058 I'm very grateful for what I have and who I know
1059 I now find the answers for which I've been searching
1060 I now choose to find all items I've lost
1061 It's okay for me to go first class all the way
1062 My life has unlimited possibilities
1063 I clear up all misunderstandings today
1064 I deserve to experience the good life in many forms
1065 I always have plenty of help whenever I need it
1066 It's okay to radically change my mind
1067 I'm free from feeling I have to hide my pain
1068 I'm free from feeling that all I have is my pain
1069 I'm always in the mood to hear good news
1070 Today belongs to me
1071 Life can always get better and it always does
1072 I'm free from crying to get what I want
1073 I'm free from using tears as a weapon
1074 I'm now aware of the kinds of words I regularly use
1075 I now choose to use more positive words
1076 My communication skills are continually improving
1077 I have many desires and it's okay to fulfill them

1078 It's okay to color outside the lines today
1079 I am freedom incarnate
1080 Today I choose my words wisely
1081 Even in dark times, I look for and find life's rainbows
1082 I'm now free from being easily provoked
1083 It's time to get back into the main stream of life again
1084 Today I open my eyes to life's endless possibilities
1085 It's okay to talk to myself
1086 It's okay to answer myself, from within
1087 I'm now free of believing in superstition
1088 I'm now done with being possessive
1089 My wedding ceremony is now turning out perfectly
1090 It's okay to get positive attention on my wedding day
1091 It's okay to get positive attention on any day
1092 I always choose the right time to express my opinions
1093 I'm now ready to reveal my talents to the world
1094 The world is now ready to accept my talents
1095 It's okay to be an orphan; the world is my family
1096 Tough times are behind me; I bless and release them
1097 I choose freedom today
1098 I now choose to be on time for everything
1099 It's okay to ignore misguided advertising
1100 Today I give up struggling against the Universe
1101 I'm imaginative and creative
1102 I enjoy being a deep thinker
1103 Being dramatic when I speak is part of who I am
1104 It's okay that I'm considered a complicated person
1105 I renounce all labels that are intended to limit me
1106 I choose to be efficient in my actions today
1107 When people tell me their feelings I listen with love
1108 I remain free from problems or worries
1109 I choose to be free from underestimating myself
1110 It's okay to be unpredictable if I choose
1111 My life is a series of great choices I've made
1112 I choose to be famous in my own lifetime
1113 I'm valuable just as I am
1114 I believe I can conquer anything today
1115 I allow wondrous things to happen to me today
1116 I see great potential in myself
1117 I always consider all possibilities

1118 Life is a game and I choose to earn extended play
1119 I now choose to be self-motivated
1120 I relate easily with others
1121 I see every challenge as an opportunity
1122 The changes that are occurring in my life feel natural
1123 Now that I'm (insert current age) I can do anything I like
1124 I'm now free from forcing issues
1125 I pay attention to all that's around me today
1126 I have a solid personality, full of depth and purpose
1127 I have brilliant ideas and it's okay to share them
1128 The decisions I make today are right for all concerned
1129 I walk and move with dignity and grace
1130 My day is filled with marvelous coincidences
1131 It's okay to be a legend in my own mind
1132 Daydreaming is productive, and I indulge in it often
1133 My physical endurance level increases daily
1134 Talking to people on the phone is now easier for me
1135 It's okay to be shy; I still get my point across
1136 I'm now giving up the need to appear shy
1137 Being shy is a part of who I am, and I accept all of me
1138 It's okay to be loud and outspoken
1139 Giving up the need to be loud and outspoken is okay
1140 Being outspoken is a part of who I am
1141 When I look in the mirror, I smile at the person I am
1142 I give up the need to prove others wrong
1143 I'm climbing to new heights concerning my self-worth
1144 I'm a delightful person to be around
1145 Terrific happenings occur in my life today
1146 This is only the beginning of the great things to come
1147 My life is now working out exactly as I wish
1148 I'm finished with focusing on disagreements
1149 I've taken the word "impossible" out of my vocabulary
1150 Everything in my world always turns out all right
1151 Realizing my true self-worth is exciting
1152 I behave as the kind of person I'd most like to be
1153 I'm able to see the positive outcomes of my decisions
1154 I'm finished with putting down my competitors
1155 My plans for my future are flexible
1156 Today I choose to treat all sales people with respect
1157 I speak kindly to all clerks, and people who serve me

1158 I choose to build up the self-esteem of others today
1159 I am emotionally self-sufficient now
1160 I choose to remember that I am always powerful
1161 I am at one with my creator 100% of the time
1162 I have given up any need for anxiety and worry
1163 I am now free from the lure of distractions
1164 I choose to be free of the trap of procrastination
1165 I remain attentive all of this day
1166 I choose to be led by the mind of God
1167 It's okay to question any of my past beliefs
1168 I continue to question my current beliefs
1169 I support only what is meaningful today
1170 I choose to break free from negative routines today
1171 I let go of all irritations today
1172 I carry blessings with me and leave them wherever I walk
1173 It's okay to let my anger dissipate now
1174 I find new ways today to put creativity into my work
1175 There's always a reason to keep on living
1176 All the events in my life contain great gifts
1177 I stay alert while driving on all trips
1178 My world is filled with beauty
1179 I choose to be generous to everyone in my world
1180 I consider all sides to issues
1181 I gently demand the best from myself and I deliver
1182 I happily do many acts of kindness today
1183 I share my bliss with the world today
1184 I remember to spend time in total silence today
1185 I'm perfectly comfortable with the decisions I make
1186 I reclaim my personal power today
1187 Today I choose to focus on my strengths
1188 I tingle with anticipation of what's ahead of me
1189 I enjoy bringing people together
1190 I have a great deal of stamina
1191 I depend upon my own good instincts
1192 I'm known as very dependable
1193 I remain detached from other people's dramas
1194 I pay attention to the details of my life
1195 I pay attention to the big picture of my life
1196 Developing new interests is something I do often
1197 It's easy now for me to avoid devious people

1198 I am a diamond and I deserve to shine
1199 I take the direct approach when solving challenges
1200 I now begin to make music in the orchestra of life
1201 I now refuse to wear any kind of personality disguise
1202 My dominant traits include love, compassion and joy
1203 I allow peaceful thoughts to dominate my consciousness
1204 Each day I have the opportunity to begin again
1205 I choose to duplicate the positive qualities of others
1206 I make all the changes that I wish, with ease
1207 It's okay to have elaborate plans for my future
1208 I choose to be free of embarrassment
1209 My capacity for change is immense
1210 I find enjoyment in living every moment
1211 My enthusiasm for living and learning is contagious
1212 I'm establishing myself as an expert on positive behavior
1213 It's all right to always expect the best
1214 It's all right to get my hopes up and I do
1215 I choose to breathe new life into my projects today
1216 I've decided it's time to get on with my life
1217 I make decisions based on what is for my own good
1218 My insurance rates continue to go down
1219 It's now time to clear my mind and soul
1220 All of my experiences have made me the person I am
1221 I choose to be punctual today and always
1222 I keep all the promises I make
1223 I am accommodating to the feelings of others today
1224 I'm now free from the tendency to overreact
1225 I am now free from worry of failure
1226 Every day my emotional baggage becomes lighter
1227 I am relaxed and productive
1228 My true beauty radiates from within my heart
1229 I choose to be supportive of myself
1230 Enemies are a figment of my imagination
1231 I choose a state of abundance today
1232 I have a great attitude
1233 Thinking clearly is a luxury I always possess
1234 I continue to remain free of delusion
1235 I am free from stereotypical comments and attitudes
1236 I choose to accept myself as I am now
1237 I choose to accept others as they are now

1238 Dedication to my causes is a good thing
1239 I am focused and powerful in this moment
1240 I remain excited about life's possibilities
1241 I'm now free from repeating past mistakes
1242 I choose to be free of embarrassing situations
1243 This city holds great promise for me
1244 Life is a big game and I've decided to win
1245 This moment is special and I treat it that way
1246 I've come a long way and I choose to remember that
1247 I'm now free from believing in limits
1248 Today I learn something that surprises and delights me
1249 Winning comes from the heart
1250 I sink my teeth into the causes that excite me
1251 It's okay if I choose to live like a hermit
1252 It's okay if I choose to live the life of a recluse
1253 I heartily welcome my positive feelings back today
1254 It's okay to choose to be unaffected by harsh words
1255 It's okay to rise above everyone's expectations of me
1256 There's always something positive left to say
1257 I'm better in this moment than I have ever been
1258 I am always protected from fear and despair
1259 I let my light shine brighter each day
1260 Telling other people's secrets is a part of my past
1261 I remember people's names with incredible accuracy
1262 It's okay to take major bursts ahead in life
1263 I'm very pleased with my life's turn of events
1264 I own my thoughts and feelings
1265 People perceive me as intelligent because I am
1266 It's okay to be charismatic
1267 I work well with all types of people
1268 I spend my money and my time wisely
1269 I'm drawn toward positive energy people
1270 I remember to rest my eyes several times today
1271 Life goes on and I'm thrilled to be a part of it
1272 Gravity and I have an understanding and are friends
1273 Men and women are now communicating more openly
1274 Judgment calls are a thing of my past
1275 T. T. F. N. (ta ta for now) negative thoughts
1276 I enjoy breathing from my gut
1277 Today I piece together more of the pattern of my life

1278 I enjoy laughing, so I choose to do it often
1279 I take one day at a time, enjoy life and share love
1280 I drop-kick my problems out of my consciousness
1281 I choose to be fascinated by self-growth
1282 I say thank you to all those who've helped me
1283 My intentions are good and so is my heart
1284 I take huge steps toward being independent today
1285 I choose to put into practice what I learn today
1286 I always have room for improvement
1287 I now know beyond any question, who and what I am
1288 This is it -- today I get the chance I've been waiting for
1289 Running away from my problems is part of my past
1290 Other people's kindness is something I deserve
1291 My future looks very bright
1292 I always have all the privacy I need
1293 I'm able to communicate with others on all topics
1294 I've given up worrying about others
1295 I'm living a memorable life
1296 Today I choose to create a little magic
1297 I've chosen to give up nagging
1298 I choose to see the beauty in every situation
1299 I choose to let a miracle happen today
1300 I allow myself to be nicer today
1301 Ideas solidify in my mind quickly, with great results
1302 It's okay to tell everything I know
1303 It's all right to reveal much of my thoughts to others
1304 I give up the notion of needing to be rescued
1305 This moment is my time, I do with it as I see fit
1306 My ideas are born in my soul
1307 I choose today to bring my mind to stillness
1308 I do everything with a sense of reverence today
1309 I give up any need to be stubborn
1310 I choose to take action where I've been hesitating
1311 I can do anything I want, right now, in this moment
1312 I recognize the deception under which I've been living
1313 I give up the idea that I'm a slave to anything or anyone
1314 My motives are always on target with my function
1315 It's okay to radically change my lifestyle
1316 In this moment, I am exactly where I want to be
1317 I'm free from any sense of loneliness

1318 I give up any ideas of being threatened
1319 This day I choose the high road
1320 All my doubts now disappear in an instant
1321 I choose to look on the bright side of things
1322 It's okay to have people help me
1323 I always treat all kinds of people with dignity
1324 I fulfill the obligations that I've made for myself
1325 It's okay to feel at home wherever I am
1326 There's always something to celebrate
1327 I enjoy being a student of life
1328 Today I discover what I'm an expert at
1329 Today I let go of the temptation to force things
1330 I'm thorough when cleaning out garbage from my mind
1331 I sail effortlessly through my tasks today
1332 I'm getting better at speaking in front of people
1333 I'm now able to sort out all of my feelings
1334 I can afford to loosen my grip on issues in my life
1335 It's okay to do something right the first time
1336 My worries are few and far between
1337 I lessen my worry thoughts every day
1338 I always find the best solutions to challenges
1339 It's okay to appear human in public situations
1340 I communicate my feelings using very few words
1341 The rules of my life change rapidly and I keep up well
1342 I'm now able to claim my space
1343 I'm always a good sport
1344 I find it easy to call people on the telephone
1345 All of my appointments go smoothly
1346 I choose for all of my "some days" to be now
1347 Complaining is part of my past and I let it go
1348 My private life remains my own
1349 I'm ready to live life to its fullest and life's ready for me
1350 It's okay to have differences of opinion
1351 Thoroughness is part of my nature
1352 I now give up any attachments to negative thoughts
1353 I respect myself for the choices I make
1354 I have a well-rounded personality
1355 It's okay to always do what I feel is right
1356 Talking with my elders is informative and fun
1357 I always speak with complete sincerity

1358 I give myself enough room to breathe
1359 Tragedy avoids me like the plague today
1360 It's a person's prerogative to change his/her mind
1361 I'm of the opinion that a life is always worth saving
1362 I'm always ready to receive insightful information
1363 The chances of my fantasies becoming realities are high
1364 Being curious is okay, it helps me learn
1365 I'm prepared for my life to change for the better now
1366 I'm enjoying the process
1367 I choose to be free from burn out
1368 I choose to focus on only positive things
1369 My world is now becoming positive
1370 I'm able to make decisions all by myself
1371 My self-worth is strong
1372 I choose to cherish myself today
1373 I always arrive to my appointments on time
1374 I enjoy spending time alone
1375 I'm done with critical thoughts of myself and others
1376 I choose to release blame from my consciousness
1377 I choose to be on time today and every day
1378 I'm free from discouraging others
1379 In all traffic, I remain calm and friendly
1380 I dismiss any murderous thoughts or tendencies
1381 I choose to live beyond quiet desperation
1382 I am now living a charmed life
1383 Decisions based on greed are in my past
1384 Each person has innate value, including me
1385 I choose and wear colors today by gut feelings
1386 I believe I can be trained to do anything
1387 I choose now to trust myself versus so-called experts
1388 My point of view is as important as anyone's
1389 I choose to live my existence in harmony at all times
1390 I recognize the good ideas of others
1391 I now have a life free of unsolicited sales people
1392 I take my attention off of anger and conflict
1393 I seek and gain attention in positive ways only
1394 I see what's going right in my life and in the world
1395 I focus on love, joy, acceptance and peace
1396 I do make a positive difference to the world
1397 My life is proof of my integrity

1398 Creativity flows from my consciousness effortlessly
1399 Today I see the birth of a new idea
1400 I experience delight in all activities today
1401 I'm able to keep my emotions balanced today
1402 I'm well known for always telling the truth
1403 I pray that in some way my life is an inspiration today
1404 I choose to be spontaneous and enjoy my existence
1405 Today I've decided to simplify my life
1406 Releasing negative thoughts is easier than I expected
1407 My world values honesty, integrity and synchronicity
1408 I surrender the need to always be in control
1409 My heart, mind and soul are filled with compassion
1410 Today I live with joyful expectancy
1411 The people in my world live in harmony
1412 I efficiently change my thought patterns now
1413 Today I choose faith as the answer to all questions
1414 I treat everyone with tenderness today and always
1415 I allow my body to shed purifying tears when necessary
1416 My existence is filled with gratitude
1417 My thought patterns go through a major transformation
1418 I release any and all feelings of stubbornness
1419 My communication skills improve rapidly now
1420 I discover my purpose within this moment
1421 I use humor appropriately today
1422 I allow my enthusiasm for life to bubble forth today
1423 Education is a part of my every day existence
1424 My life's adventures begin again now
1425 Complete freedom takes place in my heart and soul
1426 I take responsibility for my choices today and always
1427 My relationships are golden and I treat them as such
1428 Misunderstandings are cleared up easily today
1429 I exert my mental strength in all I do today
1430 I remain flexible when making decisions
1431 I remember to take time to play today
1432 I choose to relinquish judging
1433 I easily meet all deadlines
1434 I transform all thoughts of anger into amused thoughts
1435 I choose to intentionally build people up today
1436 We all have problems, so I send us all love
1437 I let my Inner Child out to play with me today

1438 I let my Inner Child hug all strangers today
1439 My wants and needs are easily met
1440 I relinquish making decisions in anger
1441 I'm through making jokes at the expense of others
1442 All is well in my world in this moment
1443 I'm through with sitting on the fence
1444 I make decisions quickly now
1445 I see only friendly faces everywhere I go
1446 My family supports me in all I do
1447 My positive feelings find their way into stubborn hearts
1448 I accept change with a positive attitude today
1449 I choose to enjoy everything I experience today
1450 I enjoy spending time with nature
1451 I choose to spend some time outdoors today
1452 I settle comfortably into the joy and possibility of today
1453 I'm finished going through any drama or turmoil
1454 I focus positive energy on an issue until I get results
1455 I attract people who look out for my best interests
1456 I give up all feelings of being betrayed
1457 I belong in the company of positive people
1458 I'm through with ruining my life
1459 I have impeccable manners
1460 I allow positive statements to positively affect me
1461 I accept the responsibility I've been given
1462 I use time to my advantage today
1463 It's okay to go back to the drawing board
1464 Facts and figures are now falling into place for me
1465 Rules in my life are made and dissolved by me
1466 I choose the pace in which I work
1467 Everywhere I go I reach out to others today
1468 I break out of my mold today
1469 I form new, positive patterns today
1470 It's okay to enjoy doing repetitive tasks
1471 I throw 4 or 5 pennies, sending good luck to others
1472 Brilliant people are drawn to me
1473 I always find trustworthy people
1474 I pray for the divine in me to shine forth today
1475 I'm now convinced that I'm a good person
1476 Ideas for personal improvement come to me quickly
1477 The shape of my future is pleasing to me

1478 I follow written and oral directions well
1479 I use my heart today to tell me when to use my mouth
1480 I now feel safe and secure and full of hope
1481 I feel the tension flowing away from my body now
1482 I crush negative thoughts beneath my feet today
1483 I see the humor in ridiculous situations
1484 It's okay for creative thoughts to take a while to process
1485 I remember to really listen to people when they speak
1486 I let go of pre-conceived notions today
1487 I love radically different parts of my personality
1488 It's a piece of cake to follow my right path in life
1489 My heart has now been altered for the good
1490 I appreciate it when people do favors for me
1491 Today I remember to write in my journal or diary
1492 I'm able to do all that I wish to accomplish today
1493 I talk less and listen more today
1494 I choose to participate wholly in my life today
1495 It's okay to have shameless fun today
1496 The time is always now to make any and all changes
1497 I choose to have tough times step aside
1498 I determine what is tough and what is easy
1499 Totally free, that's how I feel today
1500 I'm free from putting words into other people's mouths
1501 Toys are fun to play with; I'll play with some toys today
1502 I choose to continue to learn through the rest of my life
1503 It's okay for me to have a vehicle that always runs well
1504 It's okay to be the one to apologize first
1505 Today I turn off the television and turn on my mind
1506 Making what looks like hard choices helps me to grow
1507 I free myself from having to listen to raunchy jokes
1508 I choose to be free from pessimistic thoughts
1509 Within my mind is a safe haven
1510 I am kindness incarnate
1511 I still find the good in people
1512 I find time to take long walks to clear my mind
1513 I choose to celebrate new memories today
1514 I am a receptor and transmitter of light energy
1515 Being polite is a positive habit of mine
1516 I'm through with subconsciously messing up my life
1517 I always recover from any temporary set-backs

1518 I'm smart and savvy and I always land on my feet
1519 Expecting the best is now part of me
1520 I interrupt dark thoughts and replace them with light
1521 I deserve a lifetime of positive, magical experiences
1522 I've accomplished much in my life and I continue
1523 I choose to allow myself to enjoy every moment
1524 All sad times now disappear for good
1525 I'm a part of everyone and everything
1526 I'm always sensitive to the feelings of others
1527 I've decided to fix my own problems
1528 I choose now to eliminate any feelings of doom
1529 I choose now to take life less seriously
1530 I'm surrounded by sweet, wonderful people
1531 I always speak in a way people understand
1532 I accept challenges and transform them into victories
1533 I always progress emotionally in the right direction
1534 All Heaven is about to break loose
1535 Today I enable myself to take charge of my life
1536 It's okay to have the time of my life today
1537 My life is filled with breath-generatingly beautiful things
1538 It's okay to count on myself, I always come through
1539 My life is delicious and I'm savoring every mouthful
1540 I've found my place on the face of the Earth
1541 I now move on to the next phase of my life
1542 I'm calling the shots in my life now
1543 I choose to be free of living in isolation
1544 I'm clear on my life objectives
1545 It's okay to act and be confident about what I do
1546 I ignore the impulse to shut down my feelings
1547 I'm able to mind my own business today
1548 I'm through with putting people into roles
1549 I'm done thinking I know exactly what others feel
1550 I choose to give up all defensiveness
1551 I now give up the idea of needing punishment
1552 I choose to give up the idea of needing to punish others
1553 Punishment is very over-rated, so I'm through with it
1554 Guilt is very over-rated, and I release that notion now
1555 I choose to allow everything in my life to work out well
1556 Feeling strange every once in a while is all right
1557 Today is an extraordinary day

1558 I have an extreme case of good humor today
1559 I show my true self to the world today
1560 I behave in a fair manner in business dealings
1561 I get off the fence today and make a decision
1562 I've now given up all desire to be involved in a fight
1563 Verbal and physical fighting is a part of my past
1564 I find a way to make everything turn out all right
1565 I let harsh words go in one ear and out the other
1566 I speak my truth today, as my truth is important
1567 I have the confidence it takes to speak with assurance
1568 Support comes from unexpected sources today
1569 It's okay to rely on my survival skills today
1570 I change my speaking today to reflect the new me
1571 Today I choose words carefully, and consciously
1572 Endings are beginnings... always
1573 This is the best time of my life, so far
1574 This is the best day of my life, so far
1575 I sense a change of heart within my so-called enemies
1576 I discover my highest reason for living today
1577 I choose the right times to speak and to be quiet today
1578 I'm through with proving to the world how tough I am
1579 I'm complete, just as I am
1580 I let down emotional walls of resistance today
1581 I'm free from raising my voice to others today
1582 It's okay for me to be president of my own fan club
1583 I'm free from any notion of being involved in disasters
1584 Today I have a million reasons to be smiling
1585 I have great confidence in my future
1586 I've decided to cease from worry thoughts now
1587 I take good care of myself and my family
1588 Everything's going to be okay
1589 This fascinating moment is all there is, and that's okay
1590 Change happens as quickly as I allow it
1591 All the surprises in my life are positive and wonderful
1592 Soaring feelings of triumph makes my work worthwhile
1593 I reach out and touch the hand of opportunity today
1594 I walk arm in arm with my good now and always
1595 Self-confidence is part of what makes me so attractive
1596 Defenseless is the only way to be
1597 I reach deep inside myself today for the answers

1598 I'm extremely dedicated to the task at hand
1599 I respect all points of view, even if different from mine
1600 It's okay when good news happens suddenly
1601 Everyone has the capacity for positive change
1602 I choose to change for the better today
1603 I mentally flush negativity from my system today
1604 I'm always moving forward
1605 I'm full of self-confidence and assurance today
1606 I'm generous and enjoy giving to friends and strangers
1607 I quickly bounce back when negative thoughts come
1608 I choose, right now, to remain free from doubt
1609 I have my own style and I like it
1610 I'm free from being a prisoner to fashion
1611 I give away some smiles today
1612 When I sing, my spirits rise
1613 I'm always willing to try new things
1614 When the doors of opportunity open I step through
1615 Life's challenges are opportunities
1616 I look for good in potentially bad situations
1617 I'm always able to come up with new, fresh ideas
1618 I'm living wisely today to enjoy my tomorrows
1619 I count my blessings many times each day
1620 There's good in everyone, and I find it, regardless
1621 I feel serene as I take deep breaths and relax
1622 I respect the views of others
1623 Today I'm learning by listening
1624 I'm seeing exciting happenings in my life
1625 The warmth of the sunshine is healing to my body
1626 I believe smiles are contagious
1627 When life throws me a curve I bend into it
1628 I choose to follow my words with actions today
1629 I am now more sensitive to the feelings of others
1630 I have integrity and credibility
1631 I believe there's a reason for my existence
1632 My life is affecting many people in a positive way
1633 I'm exhilarated by the beauty in us all
1634 I'm learning to listen with my heart
1635 As I complete a task I feel satisfaction
1636 There's more to life than what's visual to me
1637 A soothing melody rings in my heart

1638 I'm free from being overwhelmed by demands of life
1639 I overcome all adversities
1640 Possibilities have become my realities
1641 I'm now moving into the beautiful part of my lifetime
1642 I grow more beautiful and loving each day
1643 I'm now ready to restore myself to beauty
1644 I grow healthier each moment of each day
1645 I now do what brings me bliss
1646 I am blissfully beautiful, inside and out
1647 I see the true beauty in all things
1648 It's beautiful to be wealthy, healthy and joyful
1649 I share my bounty with others
1650 I love humanity
1651 I see the beauty in humanity
1652 I unfurl my brow and relax my face muscles
1653 I let things happen at their appointed times today
1654 Ultimately I believe life is really cool
1655 I'm free from feeling danger lurking around corners
1656 It's okay to have thoughts that I quickly discard
1657 Taking good care of myself is a good idea
1658 Everything happens in perfect synchronicity
1659 I put my mind in neutral many times today, to rest
1660 I'm in total harmony with everything around me
1661 I'm in total harmony with everything within me
1662 I've given up the need and the desire to judge
1663 I choose to be free from ever being scolded again
1664 I reprogram my mind to think positive thoughts
1665 I choose to see the humor in all areas of my life
1666 I'm able to handle confrontations much better now
1667 I believe I'm able to achieve anything
1668 I choose to create positive thoughts
1669 I know that I'm heading towards my abundance
1670 When I test my survival skills, I always come out on top
1671 I allow the trouble thoughts of today to now float away
1672 Today it's okay to let myself get carried away
1673 I always ask really good questions
1674 I remember that I have a second wind
1675 I choose to accept my second wind now
1676 I choose to have a good time in my life today
1677 I am equipped to handle anything that comes up

1678 I take full responsibility for my feelings and actions
1679 I always keep my sense of humor
1680 I have unique, valuable qualities
1681 I trust what I feel in my heart
1682 It's okay to do something because it feels right
1683 I embrace and breathe into my emotions today
1684 Today I choose to have a good belly laugh
1685 Speaking my truth is a gift
1686 All of my encounters today are win/win situations
1687 It's okay for me to agree to disagree
1688 I've decided to discard all emotional masks today
1689 I've decided to be totally myself today
1690 It's okay to openly share my opinions with others
1691 Today I choose to just "get over it"
1692 Today I choose to remember I'm the creator of my life
1693 I now choose to experience the here and now
1694 Today I choose to be fully in the present moment
1695 I am now free from worrying about other people
1696 I'm now free from having other people worry about me
1697 I have confidence in my coping abilities
1698 I take responsibility for the consequences of my actions
1699 I choose my own experiences and learn from them all
1700 I trust myself to handle the outcome of every situation
1701 I'm now free from spurting out old rhetoric
1702 I'm now free from anger and depression
1703 My gut feelings are more reliable than my eyesight
1704 I now change the mistaken belief that I deserve misery
1705 Today I dance to the music that makes my heart sing
1706 I choose to find time to relax today
1707 I have chosen to be free from me-bashing today
1708 Today I choose to be free of self-induced suffering
1709 I'm now free from creating storms in my life
1710 I choose to speak my truth in a kind, yet firm manner
1711 Today I choose how to release my feelings
1712 I choose to be emotionally in balance today and always
1713 I retain my personal power when I extend love to others
1714 I'm consciously choosing to embrace and release anger
1715 Today I choose to quiet my soul
1716 Today I give myself a good conduct medal
1717 I'm free from playing hide and seek with my emotions

1718 I choose to be free from letting my life stand still
1719 I choose to be free from all problems today
1720 I keep my nose out of people's business
1721 Life is full of amazingly wonderful surprises
1722 I'm the most important thing that's ever happened to me
1723 I'm always able to take care of myself
1724 I'm back in the magic again
1725 I'm always proud of myself
1726 It's okay to do things a different way today
1727 It's okay to turn my negative thoughts into positive ones
1728 I allow my mind to explore the true depths of who I am
1729 Today I choose to gain insights into my mind
1730 I discover why I think and feel as I do on certain issues
1731 I'm beginning a new, exciting path of self-discovery
1732 It's okay to have questions without immediate answers
1733 I ignore the opinion of what society thinks I should do
1734 Today I really pay attention to my thoughts
1735 I always choose carefully the words to speak
1736 I use affirmations when confronted with tough issues
1737 I experiment, have fun, and change my life to the good
1738 I think, speak, write and communicate positively now
1739 I remember there is a never-ending supply of ideas
1740 It's okay today to share my gutsy insights
1741 I find new ways of how and when to release my anger
1742 I choose to live a wealthy existence
1743 I'm strong and healthy in mind, body and spirit
1744 Today I choose to avoid interrupting people
1745 Today I choose to monitor the tone of my voice
1746 Today I choose to state my positive intent
1747 Today I choose to use positive messages when I speak
1748 Today I choose to listen and to understand
1749 I choose now to give people the benefit of the doubt
1750 It's through new attitudes that I create new results
1751 The outcome of my life reflects my positive attitude
1752 I choose to notice my present blessings
1753 I always choose to make my attitude a good one
1754 I look inside for reasons why I feel nervous
1755 Being nervous or calm is a choice I make
1756 Today I choose to achieve the impossible
1757 My attitude propels me toward my achievements

1758 I'm doing my best I make a difference to the world
1759 Today I choose to do what people say I cannot do
1760 It's okay to feel that I'm good at what I do
1761 I am unique and will compare myself to no one
1762 Every experience in life is a lesson
1763 I take the word "failure" out of my vocabulary
1764 I am the star of the movie of my life
1765 I choose to see my life drama and release it
1766 I choose to set my sights very high
1767 I have the ability today to cooperate with others easily
1768 I recognize and appreciate my own uniqueness
1769 Believing in my perfect goodness IS being humble
1770 I can handle all changes that rapidly occur in my life
1771 I choose now to be free from taking offense
1772 I choose now to depend on forces inside myself
1773 I now look for the best in all living things
1774 My spiritual, mental and physical needs are met
1775 Within this present moment I become a better person
1776 The world deserves to hear my great ideas
1777 I now choose to believe that I am worthwhile
1778 Everything happens in its good time
1779 It's my time for prosperity now
1780 Once I set my mind to something, I consider it done
1781 I am free from creating any of my own problems today
1782 I quiet my mind and let it truly absorb positive energy
1783 Creativity happens in the present tense
1784 Today I replace worry with exhilaration
1785 I send kind and loving thoughts to anything negative
1786 I make a positive difference in the lives around me
1787 I give up any feelings of guilt
1788 I choose to flamboyantly change my attitude and my life
1789 I am thankful for what I have and for what I don't have
1790 Changing my internal world changes my external world
1791 I have the potential to be anything I want to be
1792 I'm now free from believing in scarcity
1793 I have the courage to live the life I've always imagined
1794 I am free from buying into other people's views of me
1795 I have everything I need to experience life to the fullest
1796 I have many power surges, which I accept today
1797 My life is a flower, opening in its own sweet time

1798 Today I choose to let my emotions flow freely
1799 Today I choose to do what I can... and I can do anything
1800 We're all dealt winning cards; I choose to play mine
1801 I'm now free from searching for scapegoats
1802 I'm grateful for my existence, and I give it all I've got
1803 I take care of myself physically, mentally and spiritually
1804 I find time to let my Inner Child out to play today
1805 I am more powerful than my anger
1806 It's okay to tell someone that they hurt me
1807 It's okay to tell someone I'm sorry that I hurt them
1808 It's okay to ask for what I want
1809 It's okay to ask for help when I feel I need it
1810 I see past other people's anger to their true feelings
1811 When I feel tears behind my eyelids, I let them out
1812 I see all my endings as positive experiences
1813 Finding time to be alone is an ability I now possess
1814 I expect the best from everyone today and I get it
1815 I visualize people giving me a standing ovation
1816 I do much with what I'm given
1817 I remove any mental blocks that are holding me back
1818 It's okay to remove profanity from my vocabulary
1819 I pray for emotional well-being for us all
1820 God, bless us all as one
1821 Being anonymous gives me freedom
1822 I now fulfill my life's passions
1823 I find comfort whenever and wherever I need it today
1824 I choose to be impressed with myself today
1825 Life is a barrel of laughs; today I laugh a lot
1826 In my life I concentrate on what is meant to be
1827 It's okay to calmly focus on my desired outcomes
1828 I have a heightened sense of well-being today
1829 I still believe in fairy tales with happy endings
1830 Beauty is in the eye of the positive-minded person
1831 I choose to show courtesy to everyone I meet today
1832 We are all worthy of respect, I respect everyone today
1833 Today I choose to be free from being sarcastic
1834 I show how appreciative I am to all the people in my life
1835 I pay attention to the tone of my voice and keep it loving
1836 I work on and work through any misunderstandings
1837 I love all that life has to offer, and all that I offer to life

1838 It's okay for me to aspire to greatness
1839 I find time to spend part of this day in perfect stillness
1840 I seek variety in my life today, to avoid boredom
1841 I find time today to be with my special someone
1842 I choose to give myself gentle understanding
1843 It's okay to comfort my child within
1844 Today I choose to see everyone as if for the first time
1845 I choose to receive this moment as the gift that it is
1846 It's okay to feel an old pain today, and then let it go
1847 It's okay to let go of old painful memories and feel relief
1848 Today I choose to relinquish my control over others
1849 I am free from clinging to others for emotional support
1850 It's okay to rely on myself for support
1851 It's okay to rely on God for support
1852 It's fun to notice the things that are working well
1853 I choose a healthy attitude all day today
1854 I choose to see the humor in all circumstances today
1855 Today I find the solutions to my problems
1856 Today I deserve to find all of life's solutions
1857 I choose today to give up all guilt
1858 Today I choose to slow down my pace just a bit
1859 It's okay to rest even when things are in turmoil
1860 Today I make it clear to others what my boundaries are
1861 Today I take responsibility for reclaiming my power
1862 I remain open and flexible to my opinion of others
1863 I am proud of the women in my family
1864 I am proud of the men in my family
1865 I'm proud of myself...who I am and who I am becoming
1866 I express my talent and creativity in all I do today
1867 My most important choice is accepting guidance today
1868 I release myself from any poverty consciousness
1869 It's easy for me to keep my eyes on the target
1870 It's okay to weep, and it's okay to be done weeping
1871 Today I keep my chin up and my nose down
1872 I blow away trouble thoughts now, with each breath
1873 I like that I make choices carefully, yet quickly
1874 I am free of the desire to cause trouble for others
1875 Giving makes me feel good
1876 Receiving makes me feel good
1877 I give as easily as I receive

1878 I receive as easily as I give
1879 I remember that anything I say may be repeated
1880 My memory gets better each day
1881 Being on time is one of my good traits
1882 The weather is just right today and every day
1883 I choose to give myself daily compliments
1884 Making big decisions is a rewarding experience
1885 I am a quick learner
1886 It's okay when people think I'm wrong
1887 I keep my mouth closed about people's faults
1888 One of my valuable traits is enthusiasm
1889 I have faith that we will all join in harmony
1890 Today I am wiser than yesterday
1891 I like to tell people how great they are, so I do
1892 I am able to shrug off repeated disappointments
1893 Through tireless efforts I am realizing my potential
1894 The lives I'm touching today are touching others
1895 I love walking and listening to the birds sing
1896 I am choosing productive thoughts and actions
1897 How I interpret a situation determines how I react
1898 Today I'm living tomorrow's memories
1899 My greatest accomplishment is having loving children
1900 New thoughts are emerging because my mind is clear
1901 I'm making new paths around the roadblocks
1902 I'm growing smarter by associating with intelligent people
1903 As I'm sharing I'm also receiving blessings
1904 The more I use my talents the more talented I become
1905 For my survival I'm learning to cope
1906 The time I'm investing in my child is well spent
1907 I feel better after a good day's work
1908 I feel better after a good day's nap
1909 I give myself mental and physical hugs today
1910 I remember to drink my water and stretch today
1911 When I see beauty I accept my share
1912 I easily keep my vehicle within posted speed limits
1913 Whenever possible, I take the stairs
1914 I have adequate energy and qualifications for any job
1915 I enjoy my work so much; it feels like I'm on vacation
1916 I ask my Inner Self for help with all of my decisions
1917 My sense of humor helps me during trying times

1918 Diversity keeps my life exciting
1919 I thank God that negative feelings are only temporary
1920 My life is filled with exciting surprises
1921 I'm renewing my interest in [insert hobby]
1922 I take time to appreciate simple things
1923 Love is a requirement in my life
1924 In my circle of friends, there's always room for more
1925 My life is one brush stroke away from a masterpiece
1926 It's okay if others go around me, I'm still moving forward
1927 I show my kind heart, through my kind words today
1928 I trust my judgment
1929 I stand firm in my positive convictions
1930 It's okay to claim my abundance in the path of life
1931 My spouse and I bring out the best in each other
1932 Today I have a friend who listens
1933 I love myself, at any and all ages
1934 This stage in life is an exciting time for me
1935 I reach out and discover excitement
1936 Excitement is accessible; it's up to me to reach for it
1937 Watching doors open for me is exciting
1938 Seeing God's handiwork in my life renews my faith
1939 My energy level is high, so I'm accomplishing a lot
1940 It's all right for me to rest on low energy days
1941 Stress limits my strength, so I avoid stressful situations
1942 It's my responsibility to take good care of me
1943 I'm always contributing to society
1944 I'm increasing my mobility with exercise
1945 I'm increasing my energy with exercise
1946 When I'm with exciting people, my energy rises
1947 I have a happy heart that sends forth smiles
1948 I completely relax as I give God the controls
1949 I replace earthly negativity with enlightenment today
1950 Any insulting presence, I choose now to ignore
1951 It's okay to ignite the fire under my butt today
1952 I am, and will always be, very talented
1953 It's okay to be peaceful and ambitious at the same time
1954 It's okay to relax for a couple of hours in God's arms
1955 It's okay to ramble on every once in a while
1956 It's good to hear myself talk
1957 I expose the core of my Being to the world

1958 I choose prosperity over poverty today and always
1959 I choose to relax and go to sleep
1960 It's okay to give my children control sometimes
1961 I wake up in a world free of any illusion of separation
1962 I think I'm being followed… sure enough, there's God
1963 I am free of the illusion of a cruel, fear-based God
1964 I now take any stigma off of being left-handed
1965 Being left-handed is part of what makes me unique
1966 I'm good, boy howdy, I'm really good
1967 Today is the start of something big
1968 I always finish what I start
1969 Getting older gracefully is an art that I posses
1970 I'm free from allowing distractions to bring me down
1971 Today I'll be quick to praise and slow to find fault
1972 I speak kindly with all people
1973 I dwell on positives
1974 My faith gives me a strong foundation
1975 I stay calm during a crisis
1976 What seems like a crisis, is a blessing in disguise
1977 Sometimes obstacles turn me in a better direction
1978 Some mountains of worry turn out to be little hills
1979 One key to accomplishment is desire
1980 An ingenious person makes possible that which isn't
1981 Kind words are healing
1982 Everyone can use a hug
1983 My confidence grows with each success
1984 I succeed because I'm resilient
1985 I ask my body to completely relax, and it does
1986 Tonight I allow the angels to massage my stress away
1987 I give over all of the parts of my life to God
1988 I discover new passageways today on my path
1989 I continue with my work until God feels I am done
1990 I continue with my work until I feel I am done
1991 I choose to change my perception from stress to joy
1992 It's okay to release the perception that I'm a sinner
1993 Every day we are all closer to living in a perfect world
1994 I let go of any thoughts of work as I drift off to sleep
1995 Compliments are like flowers, I give out bouquets
1996 I'm always at the ready for God's guidance and advice
1997 I am and will always be a creature of light

1998	I accept miraculous events as a normal part of my day
1999	The parts that work in my life are those I give to God
2000	I am in continual communication with my Creator
2001	I'm grateful for what I'm willing to give to God
2002	I'm in a very enjoyable time in my Earth plane existence
2003	I choose to leave the fun in today
2004	I choose to get a good night's sleep tonight
2005	It's okay to ask my children for help, they enjoy giving it
2006	I visualize my desired outcome and release it to God
2007	Today I look within to find the answers to my questions
2008	Today I choose to be daring and try new things
2009	Today I choose to be daring and try new thoughts
2010	It's okay to see where I've been, and where I am now
2011	The healing's the thing
2012	I figure out new ways to motivate myself
2013	I accept my power and the responsibility with it
2014	I now see my beautiful life unfolding before my eyes
2015	I easily stay connected to my divine energy source
2016	It's okay to put my 2 cents into a conversation
2017	Like a genie, I can change reality in the blink of an eye
2018	Today I choose to question everything
2019	Today I choose to question nothing
2020	My genuine goodness is always a part of me
2021	I now refuse to allow germs to enter my body
2022	I continue to lose weight and gain knowledge
2023	I believe men and women are equally great drivers
2024	I'm now free from being a workaholic
2025	I'm able to keep a positive attitude, even at work
2026	I'm now free from feeling put down by others
2027	I'm free from all addictions now
2028	Today I choose out of deceiving myself
2029	Today I choose to lose my rigidity in all situations
2030	How I treat myself determines how others treat me
2031	I now make positive changes
2032	Today I choose to release my fear
2033	I love to feel completely relaxed, so I indulge in it often
2034	I give my body over to complete relaxation
2035	I'm successful and valuable when doing work I love
2036	I'm successful and valuable when I'm breathing
2037	Seeing others as my equals is becoming easier

2038 At birth I'm given all the tools I need to succeed
2039 I find some meaning to my life today
2040 We are all miracles
2041 I choose to be inspired today
2042 I am fair and kind and generous
2043 I'm taken seriously in life, no matter what I weigh
2044 God, I accept your healing in this moment
2045 There's a certain beauty in the ritual of folding clothes
2046 I choose now to reconnect with the moment
2047 Today I choose to follow my guides..... inward
2048 I have lots of energy at my fingertips today
2049 I watch the ooze of hate be replaced by the river of love
2050 My soundest investment is my health
2051 I do myself a favor when I help someone else
2052 I give my full attention to the one who is speaking to me
2053 I am pleased with pictures of myself
2054 My ideas are only worthwhile when I put them into action
2055 When I love what I'm doing, it isn't work
2056 I am able to undertake and complete any task
2057 Charm and courtesy are valued traits
2058 Good friends exchange unselfish deeds
2059 I am AT peace, I am IN peace, I am WITH peace
2060 What I admire in others is what I admire in me
2061 I choose what to hide or show to the world
2062 It's possible to rest in peace and still be living
2063 My mind is so clear I can see through it
2064 An idea that will help humanity is coming to me now
2065 I share my sleep time with my Creator
2066 I'm thankful for the warm home I live in
2067 I pray for the homeless
2068 I am part of the great big world around me
2069 I'm now free from any ringing in my ears
2070 I'm now free from insomnia
2071 I have the patience of all the saints
2072 I notice all that I accomplish from my to do list
2073 I am a Princess, my crown is made of light
2074 I love and forgive myself now, today and always
2075 I continue my affirmation training throughout my life

Addictions / Negative Habits

My opinion is that we all have some sort of addiction. Some of us have more tendencies towards addictions than others, but we all have them. I was addicted to cigarettes in the past... smoked over a pack a day for many years. Thankfully I've been off of them for 14 years.   I'm still in the clutches of my food addiction, that I am working on now. Don't be ashamed to admit you have addictions, and don't be ashamed to do something positive about stopping them. They no longer have to have a hold over us.

2076 I stop my addiction to caffeine today
2077 I am free from obsessions and addictions of all kinds
2078 I easily refuse drugs of any kind
2079 In this moment I choose to remain free of alcohol
2080 I easily steer clear of smoking and second-hand smoke
2081 I release any judgments about smokers and addicts
2082 It's fun to be sober
2083 It's okay to be sober when others are not
2084 12-step programs work well for me
2085 I now have a healthy attitude about alcohol
2086 I abstain from drinking alcoholic beverages
2087 I have chosen to relinquish alcohol
2088 I enjoy the taste of fruit and vegetable juices
2089 I drink seltzer water when in a bar situation
2090 I'm now free from any eating disorder
2091 I'm now free from using caffeine-laden foods and drinks
2092 Support groups are helpful and I find just the one I need
2093 There are ways to have fun and I choose sober ways
2094 I have what's necessary to be free of smoking
2095 I have the determination to be free of alcohol
2096 Any drugs I have taken, I release out of my body
2097 I am free from grinding my teeth
2098 I'm free from all temptations to do addictive substances

2099 Biting my nails is part of my past, and I release it now
2100 I am free of any nervous habits
2101 I choose out of negative habits
2102 It's my choice to be free of cigarettes
2103 The addiction to cigarettes has left my consciousness
2104 Chain-smoking is a habit from which I am now free
2105 I release any compulsive and addictive habits
2106 Swearing is part of my past and I release that habit
2107 I am now free from the need or desire to swear
2108 Choosing to stop smoking is something I'm proud of
2109 I have the right to be smoke-free
2110 I choose smoke-free partners easily
2111 I train my children regarding nicotine and other drugs
2112 Old negative habits are easily discarded by me
2113 I now easily visualize myself as a non-smoker
2114 I'm free from letting my old habits reappear
2115 I now release my old habit of wasting time
2116 I'm now free from the desire to drink and drive
2117 I've given up the need to be lazy
2118 I've given up the need to be overly busy
2119 I give up the habit of talking too much or too little
2120 Overworking is a part of my past, and I relinquish it
2121 I've decided to quit whining today and from now on
2122 I relinquish any unconscious negative habits
2123 I am free from any thought of ever taking drugs
2124 I'm now free from the desire to take drugs
2125 I choose to be free from the desire to be drunk
2126 The desire to drink alcohol appeals to me less
2127 I choose to remain free from alcohol's influence
2128 It's now time for me to end my period of smoking
2129 I'm free from effects of cigarettes, tobacco and smoke
2130 I appreciate the lack of smoke I now have in my life
2131 I appreciate that I'm always able to breathe fresh air
2132 Today I notice a marked improvement in my health
2133 My breath control gets better and better each day
2134 I choose out of smoking

Bodily Upkeep

Forget to brush and floss your teeth? Nonsense.
Well... maybe.... We have the best of intentions to
keep our hygiene habits in check, and to take good care
of our bodies. But as the years go by, sometimes we let
a few things slide... then a few more, until all of a
sudden we've become a different person, who looks
and acts less excited about life. Get excited again
today! Go through these affirmations and see how
many of them could improve how you feel about (and
treat) your body.

2135 My posture is always perfect and comfortable
2136 Drinking cleansing water is becoming a healthy habit
2137 I deserve to be fit and healthy
2138 My body always functions perfectly
2139 I love my body and my body loves me
2140 I always treat my body with love and respect
2141 My eyesight improves daily
2142 My body performs in a healthy way 100% of the time
2143 I have power over my body, and I treat it with respect
2144 My body and my Self are a team
2145 My body is my friend
2146 I am proud of the condition of my body at all times
2147 I am thankful for the state of health my body is in
2148 I love my body more every day
2149 My body retains its beautiful shape forever
2150 It's easy for me to choose the correct foods
2151 Exercise is something I enjoy
2152 My teeth and gums remain healthy
2153 My mind works with my body
2154 I love to feel my body move
2155 My body feels and looks great
2156 My body responds well to vitamins and minerals
2157 My body enjoys healthy food for fuel

2158 My body responds well to physical exercise
2159 I deserve to be around healthy people
2160 My body easily eliminates toxins regularly
2161 My spine always stays strong and supple
2162 I enjoy engaging in physical play every day
2163 I view daily exercises as a fun activity
2164 All of my cells and organs are peaceful
2165 I deserve to have clear lungs and a strong heart
2166 I love and respect all parts of my body
2167 I feed my body only nutritional food and drink
2168 My nerves are my friends
2169 Every cell in my body relaxes and listens for guidance
2170 I love and respect all my facial features
2171 My eyes are the perfect size, shape and color for me
2172 My nose is just the right size and shape for my face
2173 My heart functions perfectly at all times
2174 I appreciate my strong, powerful heart
2175 My heart gets stronger every day
2176 I love hearing my heart beat
2177 My heartbeat holds the rhythm of my being
2178 My blood runs through my veins easily
2179 My pancreas is a part of me and I bless it
2180 I thank my lungs for the great job they do
2181 My sense of smell remains keen
2182 Every day I become more limber
2183 My workout regimen provides me with joy
2184 I take air in my lungs easily
2185 The shape of my body pleases me
2186 I pray for my continued good health
2187 I relax every cell and muscle in my body
2188 Every day my muscles become stronger
2189 I truly care about the person inside this body
2190 I'm happy to have chosen to live this life in this body
2191 I feel peace entering every cell and organ of my body
2192 My hair grows longer and more luxurious every day
2193 My nails grow longer and stronger each day

2194 I'm free from under-arm odor and sweating
2195 I heal my body in this moment
2196 I am comfortable within my body
2197 I'm the architect of my body and of my life
2198 My ears hear what they need to hear today
2199 My eyes see what they need to see today
2200 I say what must be said today
2201 I feel at home in my body
2202 I enjoy getting my teeth cleaned
2203 I remember to go to the dentist
2204 I now have the body I've always wanted
2205 My hair continues to grow lush and healthy
2206 My body has the proper balance of all nutrients
2207 I retain excellent hearing
2208 My body is my dear friend and I treat it with respect
2209 It's all right to keep the face and body I want
2210 I remember to rest when my body needs it
2211 My body enjoys walking and I do it often
2212 I learn more about my body each day
2213 The organs in my body behave at optimal levels
2214 My sinuses remain clear and functioning properly
2215 My body is easily able to digest all kinds of foods
2216 My body is now free from receiving bug bites
2217 My lungs fill with air easily and fully
2218 I remember to moisturize my body every day
2219 I stay in great physical shape my entire life
2220 I now release my body from any sensation of pain
2221 My body is free from pain and strange sensations
2222 My respiratory system always works perfectly
2223 My nervous system always works perfectly
2224 My endocrine system always works perfectly
2225 My skeletal system always works perfectly
2226 My reproductive system always works perfectly
2227 My urinary system always works perfectly
2228 My hormones are always at a perfect level
2229 My kidneys always function properly

2230 My prostate numbers are always within good levels
2231 I thank my blood cells for delivering oxygen
2232 Today I thank my liver for the great job it does
2233 I remember to give myself regular breast exams
2234 All organs and cells of my body work in harmony
2235 I thank my strong, beautiful heart for pumping life
2236 I thank my spectacular lungs for breathing life
2237 My body regularly gets all the rest it needs
2238 My sinuses drain nicely now
2239 I choose to talk myself happy today
2240 I choose loving dreams and sleep for my body
2241 I listen to my body's needs today
2242 My body and my spirit are blending more today
2243 I enjoy going to the gym and do it often
2244 The cells and organs of my body are in perfect health
2245 After a brisk walk my body is radiating health
2246 I make exercise a part of my daily routine
2247 I use my eyes to help convey my love for humankind
2248 I choose to respect and cherish my body today

Career Challenges

"If I could just punch that stupid boss of mine in the kisser I'd feel so much better…" Who hasn't thought something like this at one time or another? But of course thoughts like that just make US feel awful. Focus a bit more consciously, and lovingly, and you may find that old cranky boss turning into a big, nice softy.

Our careers are important to us. They can cause us to feel joy or to feel stress. Focusing on what we WANT in our careers (instead of what we don't want), is a powerful way to make our careers into what we choose.

2249 I receive praise from co-workers and friends
2250 My boss and I speak the same language
2251 I always explain my views clearly and calmly
2252 I trust my boss and my boss trusts me
2253 I'm the boss over my attitude
2254 My supervisor is perfect for me
2255 I can work at a different pace than my co-workers
2256 My boss sees me as an integral part of the team
2257 My good work is noticed by my supervisors today
2258 It's my turn to dazzle the boss today
2259 I remember to thank my boss and co-workers today
2260 I treat my boss and co-workers as I wish to be treated
2261 My whole office has improved moods today and always
2262 I love my job and the people with whom I work
2263 The time has come for me to accept praise
2264 Judging my boss and co-workers is part of my past
2265 I'm through competing with myself, others and time
2266 I've decided to be a positive influence on my co-workers
2267 I smile and say hello to everyone I see at work today
2268 I remember to compliment my boss and co-workers
2269 My boss now knows I can handle more responsibilities

2270 Seeing me through my boss' eyes is helpful to me today
2271 It's okay to think of my co-workers as family
2272 I treat my boss with respect today, no matter what
2273 I'm the kind of boss I always wanted to have
2274 I ask God's help before making any decision
2275 Criticism is of the past; I choose to uplift my workers
2276 I choose to astonish my co-workers by staying happy
2277 Every day I become more confident at what I do
2278 I deserve to be successful doing work I love
2279 It's okay to get paid for doing what I love
2280 My work is completed in a timely, organized fashion
2281 The quality of my work reflects who I am
2282 My work gives me more energy
2283 I'm the one all of my colleagues trust
2284 I'm very organized
2285 My original thinking helps me in my chosen career
2286 My love for my work shows
2287 It's okay to be great at what I do for a living
2288 I make a very good living
2289 I absolutely adore my work
2290 I'm on the rise to the top
2291 Every project I touch today works out well
2292 It's okay to have a job when others don't
2293 Changing careers is risk-free for me
2294 My work brings great meaning to my life
2295 Having passion for my work is natural and healing
2296 All of my work is acceptable
2297 My work flows naturally from me
2298 I'm an expert in my chosen profession
2299 My work is divinely inspired
2300 I easily produce error-free work
2301 My skills are in demand
2302 My career is going one way – to the top
2303 I'm thrilled I've found the perfect career that I love
2304 My career is an important part of who I am
2305 I return home safely from all business trips

2306 I always meet and beat deadlines
2307 I'm passionate about what I do for a living
2308 I know which direction to take in my career path
2309 I'm certain to reach the top of my field
2310 I deserve a promotion and I get it
2311 I easily become a successful entrepreneur now
2312 It's okay to live my fondest dreams
2313 The work I love is also financially rewarding
2314 I always have pleasant work surroundings
2315 It's okay to be proud of my work and myself
2316 I salute competitors for their ingenuity and send love
2317 I'm as qualified as everyone else
2318 I'm the right one to get the job done
2319 I'm constantly climbing to the top in my profession
2320 I make a living doing what makes my heart sing
2321 All work is good work, when I am joyful
2322 I adore, and am at home with, my working conditions
2323 I'm now able to concentrate on getting my work done
2324 It's okay to choose the type of career I want
2325 I choose the hours and working environment I want
2326 It's okay to enjoy being a housewife
2327 It's okay to enjoy being a househusband
2328 I enjoy my work and it shows
2329 I'm a powerhouse in my field
2330 I'm thrilled by the amount of work I get done today
2331 I remain calm while completing my work
2332 It's okay to get a big high from getting my work done
2333 I'm doing some of my most important work ever
2334 I put the fun back into my work today
2335 I completely relax when I take time off from work
2336 I stay easily and calmly caught up at work
2337 I bring up ideas today that are appreciated
2338 I easily keep my focus on the task at hand
2339 All my business and personal tasks are fun today
2340 I have wildly creative ideas today
2341 I show myself and others my creativity and intellect

2342 My positive feelings toward work are catching
2343 It's fun to go to work
2344 It's exciting to do a job well, and I excel today
2345 I have energy to perform all aspects of my job
2346 My job is an important aspect of my life's journey
2347 I function well at all job duties
2348 I calmly complete projects at work today
2349 The time spent at my job is filled with joyful times
2350 I easily reach new levels of job advancement
2351 I'm well prepared now to succeed at work
2352 I bring my Inner Child to work with me today
2353 I'm devoted and dedicated to the career I love
2354 I enjoy excelling in my career so I do it often
2355 Being committed to my job brings me joy
2356 My job gives me a feeling of satisfaction
2357 I always dress appropriately for where I work
2358 Looking professional is an option I choose today
2359 I remember to eat healthfully at work today
2360 I easily complete my work today, on time
2361 I'm becoming more fascinated with my job daily
2362 I enjoy showing my talents and skills at work today
2363 I choose to be an excellent worker today
2364 This is the day I get my raise
2365 In silence I receive my best ideas
2366 I plug into my creative energy source when at work
2367 I have energy to spare at work today
2368 I enjoy my travel to and from work every day
2369 I've decided it's the nature of my business to be fair
2370 I see men and women as equals in the business world
2371 I'm free from all mental blocks today
2372 I make decisions accurately, quickly, with assurance
2373 I'm friendly when answering others' questions
2374 I ask all pertinent questions as I receive projects
2375 My work speaks for itself
2376 My work speaks well of me
2377 I calmly voice my opinions at work today

2378 My office remains free of sick building syndrome
2379 My work and everyone's work is divinely inspired
2380 I have a great future ahead of me in my career
2381 My work, my play and my joy are tightly intertwined
2382 I now believe I'm the perfect person for this job
2383 My work is my friend and we are a good team
2384 Loving my work, it's what God intended
2385 I'm free from allowing work to overwhelm me
2386 I always find ways to keep my work interesting
2387 I am meant to finish my current projects on time
2388 Regardless of my profession, I am treated with respect
2389 Regardless of my profession, I treat myself with respect
2390 I'm in love with my work
2391 I'm a team player and I'm needed in my position
2392 I work well alone, and my boss trusts me

Charity Work

Charity begins in the home. And yet, there are also so many others who would appreciate your love and help. If you feel you currently can't help charities financially or physically, at least take a few moments to send them help with a positive energy focus.

I have many charities I enjoy helping: Heifer.org, AIDS foundation and St. Jude's Children's Hospital. If you'd like to be able to give money as well, do some prosperity affirmations with the intention firmly in mind that you want to use some of that money to send to your favorite charities. It's amazing how much quicker money appears when it has some fun and worthwhile places to go.

2393 I salute all who give time and money to charities
2394 I easily find time to donate my services to charities
2395 I have money to give generously to those in need
2396 Today I discover I have a charitable heart
2397 I now find the perfect charity to support
2398 Time spent doing charity work is time well spent
2399 I enjoy feeling needed; charities need me
2400 I let God lead me to charities that match my skills
2401 I send love today to all people in charge of charity work
2402 I send love, light and energy to all charity workers
2403 May our charitable hearts all join together in love today
2404 I take care of myself as I take care of my charity work
2405 I easily find time in my schedule for charity work
2406 Humanity begins to play its part in supporting charities
2407 Helping one another is what's going to heal this world
2408 I'm able to provide hope for any who are suffering
2409 I have time to teach another person the joy of reading
2410 I help my community by offering my skills and time
2411 Taking the time to visit with the elderly comes easily

Courage / Strength

What image comes to mind here? It has to be the beloved Lion from Wizard of Oz. "Cccccourage" is something we all can choose more often. Remember… everyone feels nervous and afraid. Having courage is to feel that fear and take a deep breath (do a few affirmations) and continue to walk forward.

2412 My courage is always with me
2413 I remain strong
2414 Today I have the courage to say hello to everyone I see
2415 I now have the strength to survive any disappointment
2416 My strength is an attribute
2417 It's okay to be strong
2418 It's okay to have strong opinions and to voice them
2419 On a daily basis, I grow stronger
2420 I feel emotionally strong
2421 I feel strong in all situations
2422 I feel the strongest I have in a long time
2423 I breathe in strength
2424 I'm strong enough to be myself, even in public
2425 I have the strength to face what's happening now
2426 All the true strength I possess comes from love
2427 I am strong and courageous
2428 I give and receive strength and comfort today
2429 I have the courage to wear whatever I want
2430 I have great moral courage
2431 I have the courage to show more of who I truly am
2432 It's okay to act brave until I feel brave
2433 I have the courage now to face the rest of my life
2434 One of the things I love about myself is my courage
2435 I retain courage and bravery even into the darkest night
2436 When I feel uncomfortable it helps me to grow stronger
2437 It's okay to choose when to be brave
2438 I choose to realize how brave I really am

Depression

Go on, admit it. Aren't we ALL depressed from time to time? In the knowing that we all allow ourselves to feel down sometimes, is also the joy of knowing we all have a way out of it…through our thoughts, beliefs and actions. Take positive action and talk lovingly and in an uplifting way to yourself today, and maybe, just maybe, life will look a bit brighter when you're through.

2439 I now choose to be free of depression
2440 I understand that it's depressing to be depressed
2441 I give over all my depression thoughts to the Universe
2442 I accept advice from God on my depression
2443 My depression melts as I return to this present moment
2444 I send the depressed part of me love today
2445 I choose to be free of depression now and forever
2446 Today I find the way out of my depression
2447 Focusing on the present moment lightens depression
2448 The present moment holds only joy
2449 Depressing thoughts now flee my mind forever
2450 Depression is a disease I give over to the Universe
2451 I know I can get better; today I choose to
2452 As I take a deep breath, I feel my depression lifting
2453 I drop all depression from my consciousness
2454 Depression does not give me a payoff, so I let it go
2455 Depression is an old habit I now relinquish
2456 I send the point of depression within my body, love
2457 All forms of depression leave me today
2458 My depression is gone and peace now surrounds me
2459 I'm now living a peaceful, depression-free existence
2460 I allow Higher Self to help me shake off my depression
2461 I set my depression aside for a while today
2462 I fully embrace my depression and allow it to heal
2463 Even short periods without depression are healthy
2464 I remember what it feels like to be free of depression

2465 I move away from depression, toward joy with each step
2466 The time I spend on the earth plane is precious
2467 I choose to spend my time on Earth in peace
2468 It's okay to be peaceful when others are depressed
2469 I now free myself from having to live out my nightmares
2470 Depression is exhausting; I choose to be energized
2471 Depression and I part company today
2472 Depression has lost its allure; I now choose peace
2473 I am responsible for freeing myself from depression
2474 I throw water on my depression and watch it melt

Disabilities

We all have disabilities.   The challenges we have in our lives give us character and allow us to grow. Some disabilities are visible to the eye, others are not. I encourage you to be easy on yourself, and others, and realize we are all dealing with forms of a disability or dysfunction, and we are all doing the best we can within this moment. Take the time today to focus positively on this…for yourself and others.

2475 Whatever my disability, I perform my job perfectly
2476 I choose to consider my disability an attribute
2477 I'm labeled with a disability, yet I have many abilities
2478 I choose to overcome all of my disabilities today
2479 Being in a wheelchair is part of what makes me unique
2480 I'm enjoying my life in spite of physical limitations
2481 I see there are gifts within each disability
2482 I am, and see myself as, a whole person
2483 I see through the disability and see myself as a person
2484 I see through others' disabilities and see them as whole
2485 I look through my disability and see the divine within
2486 We all have disabilities; mine are just physical
2487 I am a kind and gentle person
2488 I have chosen to retain my sense of humor, even now
2489 I relax, embrace and fully experience my life
2490 I release myself from fear about my disability

Divorce / Broken Relationships

Did you know that I'm the all-time expert of divorce? Sometimes it feels that way. I've been married and divorced twice, and am now in a wonderful committed relationship that has outlasted them both.

Please believe me when I say that there IS hope after divorce, and there is a tremendous amount of growth you can claim during the entire process. Is it always easy? Absolutely not. Is there always room for something positive? Absolutely. Keep as much open-mindedness and love in your divorce or break up as you can, and you will come out of it a much wiser, more loving soul.

2491 I remain happy, whether married or single
2492 It's okay to be divorced
2493 I forgive my ex-spouse
2494 I heal and bless the entire divorce experience
2495 I'm a success at getting through this period of my life
2496 It's okay to be peaceful during the divorce process
2497 I always treat our children with love
2498 I know my ex-spouse is a loving human being
2499 I forgive myself for getting divorced
2500 My ex and I are equal in the eyes of God
2501 My relationship with my ex is improving daily
2502 It's okay to retain a friendship with my ex-spouse
2503 I release all negativity surrounding my divorce
2504 I give the relationship over to the Universe
2505 I have an ex who always picks up our kids on time
2506 I have an ex who leaves me alone when I want to be
2507 My ex always pays child support, and on time
2508 My ex and I agree on the amount of child support
2509 I send peace, love and light to my ex today
2510 I give to God resentment over paying child support

2511 However I react to my ex, I'm still a good person
2512 I'm always peaceful when speaking with my ex
2513 There is a bright spirit within my ex and I see that now
2514 Any troubles I've had with my ex I release now
2515 I'm now free of any residual anger toward my ex
2516 I keep positive when in the company of my ex
2517 I deserve to have a friendly ex
2518 I've decided to be a friendly ex
2519 I'm through with anger and frustration with my ex
2520 The way I see my ex is a reflection of how I view myself
2521 I'm through with bad-mouthing my ex
2522 It's okay to be happily single
2523 The anger I've held toward my ex is now dissipating
2524 Being single brings me great happiness
2525 Being a divorcee is just part of who I am
2526 I'm okay with the fact that my ex is dating again
2527 I'm through bad-mouthing my children's father/mother

Energy

ENERGY! Is there a more important focus? According to Quantum Physics, when at our most basic ingredient, everyone and everything is pure energy. Work with energy. FEEL what it feels like to have low-energy, and then do some affirmations and notice the change in how you feel. FEEL the high energy you begin to attract and create within you, and remind yourself you deserve to continue to feel this heightened sense of being alive.

2528 I attract positive energy like a magnet
2529 Energy and strength come from my heart today
2530 I accept energy freely
2531 I extend loving energy to others today
2532 I keep my energy level high
2533 I perform with high levels of energy today
2534 I retain my high energy even through trying times
2535 I shrug off any negative energy that comes my way
2536 Whatever I eat gets converted to energy
2537 My positive energy always cancels out any negative
2538 My positive energy permeates everything I do
2539 I concentrate my energy on improving my life
2540 My consciousness attracts positive energy
2541 I walk with lots of energy and pep to my step
2542 Focusing my energies works well for me
2543 I now choose to have lots and lots of energy
2544 I always expend my energy well
2545 I draw in my scattered energies and focus well now
2546 I gather my energy to help me complete my project
2547 The more energy I give, the more I receive
2548 I have plenty of energy for all I have planned
2549 I choose to abstain from creating negative energy
2550 All thoughts are equal, I choose positive thoughts
2551 I stop moving and allow my body to re-energize.
2552 Beginnings and endings share bursts of energy

2553 Today I choose to give energy to positive situations
2554 I'm now free of wasting energy
2555 I smile and send love around negative-energy people
2556 I transform any evil energy into good energy
2557 I choose to put lots of energy into observation today
2558 I choose to be free of energy-wasting doubt
2559 I am energized today because I choose to be

Entrepreneurs

Hate your boss? Don't hold onto that feeling long, for you're about to become your own boss, and you don't need any self-hate going on. With new businesses (and at-home workers) starting every day, it's important to stay positive during the process of creating your new life. Do what you love, stay in the moment, and watch for signs on which way to go on the path to your success. Doing affirmations along the way greatly improves your focus onto your businesses success!

2560 I deserve to start my own business
2561 The fear of starting my own business is now gone
2562 Time spent working on my business is time well spent
2563 People in the community open their arms to me
2564 I make new clients quickly and easily for my business
2565 I'm now building my clientele daily
2566 I easily learn how to promote my business online
2567 I'm great at finding just the right people to help me
2568 I'm great at attracting the right clients to my business
2569 I now find the perfect employees for my company
2570 I reach a profit in a very short amount of time
2571 I send competitors love
2572 The Universe sends me business
2573 There is enough room on the planet for my company
2574 I enjoy the entire process of starting my own company
2575 I easily get any loans I need to help my business along
2576 It's okay to be proud to be a business owner
2577 I have what it takes to succeed as an entrepreneur
2578 My confidence in my abilities grows daily
2579 I always treat my workers with respect and dignity
2580 My business makes a positive difference in the world
2581 The Universe supports the growth of my business
2582 I easily juggle both my business and family lives
2583 I feel alive and energized when working in my company

Fear

YIKES! Just the word "fear" makes us want to back away, doesn't it? And yet our fears hold great insights for us on where we are focusing our thoughts, and how we feel about ourselves, and life. Fears are not bad. They point us in the direction of where we have hidden some great treasure within ourselves! Take a deep breath and go towards your fears, with lots of that courage we spoke of earlier, and then allow the fears to fall away, and the treasures to remain.

2584 My fear-based thoughts are now gone for good
2585 It's okay to talk about things that scare me
2586 I choose out of any fear-based thoughts today
2587 I am free of the fear of success
2588 I am free of the fear of failure
2589 It's okay to fear facing my fears
2590 I choose to release any fears I have about God
2591 Every day I decrease my fears
2592 I refuse to let my courage be smothered by fear
2593 I catch myself before I react through fear
2594 I watch my fear thoughts as they fly out the window
2595 Insecurity and fear are notions in my past that I release
2596 I'm now conquering my fears one at a time
2597 I'm now through with scaring myself
2598 I ask fear to gently step aside
2599 Terror has loosened its grip on my heart and I am free
2600 Things that look frightening are truly only illusion
2601 It's okay to release my fear of love
2602 I now let fear propel me toward love
2603 I now choose love and peace instead of fear
2604 I've chosen to be free from fear of the dark
2605 I am fearless
2606 I happily relinquish all fear-based thoughts
2607 My life is terror-free

2608 I choose out of fear today and always
2609 My fears decrease each day
2610 I easily allay my doubts and fears
2611 Fear takes a backseat to the peace I enjoy
2612 I am free from all forms of fear
2613 I am fearless today and always
2614 With an easy breath, I blow away my fear thoughts
2615 I face my fears and stare them down today
2616 I embrace my fears, show them love, and heal them
2617 I am free from being scared of anything
2618 I gain ground over my fears today
2619 I am free from fear of bodily injury
2620 I'm free from the fear of going to the dentist
2621 It's all right to choose out of being petrified
2622 I've now found the tools to release my fear thoughts
2623 I enjoy airline travel
2624 I'm now free of the fear of flying
2625 I'm now free of the fear of water
2626 I'm now free of the fear of heights
2627 I'm now free of the fear of _____ (fill in the blank)
2628 Today I choose to be free of the fear of death
2629 I release any fears that I have about myself
2630 It's okay to admit that I'm scared, and find my fears
2631 I put fear in its place and myself back in control
2632 Today I use faith to conquer my fears

Forgiveness

It's been said that sending others bad thoughts and then expecting to not feel badly yourself, is like drinking poison and expecting the other person to die from it. Forgiveness is primarily FOR YOU. How do YOU want to feel in life? If you think it's worth the payoff to feel awful towards someone or something in life, then go for it. Me? I'd rather forgive others (and myself) and feel joy. Do a few affirmations, and see if you start feeling more joyful too!

2633 I forgive the actions of those I feel have wounded me
2634 I forgive myself for all I feel I've done
2635 I allow myself to be forgiven
2636 I forgive my parents
2637 I forgive what I've done to the life I've been given
2638 I forgive myself for believing in old thought patterns
2639 Forgiveness comes easily to me
2640 I send forgiveness to the entire world
2641 I feel and accept forgiveness from the world
2642 Forgiving others makes me feel good
2643 Forgiving myself feels good and right
2644 It's okay to forgive myself
2645 It's okay to be guilt-free
2646 It's okay to be forgiven
2647 I deserve total forgiveness
2648 I forgive myself completely
2649 I am forgiven
2650 I forgive humanity
2651 I forgive myself for anything I've done badly to my kids
2652 I'm sorry for anything bad I've ever done
2653 I choose to forgive myself
2654 I choose to forgive my children
2655 I choose to forgive the Universe
2656 I choose to forgive my perception of God

2657 I choose to forgive my neighbors
2658 I forgive and release my childhood and its memories
2659 I forgive myself for being angry
2660 I forgive my body when it seems to fail me
2661 I forgive myself for having doubts
2662 I let go of any mistakes I've made and forgive myself
2663 I forgive myself for any times I've acted unloving
2664 I am ready to forgive myself today
2665 I am ready to forgive my parents today
2666 I am ready to forgive my children today
2667 I am ready to forgive the Universe today
2668 I forgive myself for having had an abortion
2669 I forgive myself for hating my parents
2670 I forgive myself for hating my children
2671 I forgive myself for murdering a human being
2672 I forgive myself for raping or violating a human being
2673 Forgiveness is a virtue I possess in great abundance
2674 Forgiveness is important to the future of the world
2675 I forgive, therefore I am
2676 I forgive myself for not wanting to forgive
2677 I forgive myself for thinking I'm unable to forgive
2678 I forgive myself for choosing negative responses
2679 I forgive what I've become
2680 I forgive what I haven't become
2681 I forgive my judgments over others
2682 I forgive myself for when I'm disappointed
2683 I forgive myself for when I'm angry and hostile
2684 I forgive myself for when I ignore the positive
2685 I forgive myself for hating and/or fearing God
2686 I forgive myself for caring what others think of me
2687 Forgiving myself allows me to discover my inner self
2688 Forgiveness frees up energy to use for other projects
2689 Forgiveness makes it easier to communicate with all
2690 Forgiveness is its own reward
2691 Forgiveness provides a great gift -- peace
2692 I forgive the Universe now, in this moment

2693 Everyone forgives me this day
2694 I forgive myself for ignoring who I am
2695 I forgive myself for being annoyed
2696 I forgive myself for buying into another's attitude
2697 I forgive myself for letting others push my buttons
2698 I forgive myself for pushing other people's buttons
2699 I forgive myself for ignoring God's bread crumbs
2700 I forgive myself for being tired
2701 Forgiveness is a part of my nature
2702 Forgiveness is my first reaction to any situation
2703 Forgiveness makes me smile
2704 I have a very forgiving nature
2705 It feels natural for me to forgive regularly
2706 I forgive myself for being nervous
2707 I forgive me for thinking bitter thoughts about my friends
2708 I forgive myself for any promises I've broken
2709 I forgive myself for my feelings of envy or jealousy
2710 I forgive those who speak in anger
2711 In my life, I emphasize love and forgiveness
2712 I choose to understand what forgiveness really means
2713 I forgive myself for feeling like I'm alone
2714 I choose to forgive myself for old, limiting beliefs
2715 I forgive what I perceive to be bad drivers
2716 Forgiveness is the greatest gift I give anyone today
2717 I'm relieved to discover that I'm kind and forgiving
2718 Happiness stems from loving and forgiving myself
2719 I let go of the past and correct the present
2720 I choose to freely forgive anyone I'm angry with
2721 I shorten the time it takes to forgive myself today
2722 Today I forgive other people for being human
2723 I forgive my mistakes, and the mistakes of others
2724 Today I take charge of my life by choosing to forgive
2725 The choice to heal and forgive is always mine
2726 Choosing to forgive begins the process of healing
2727 It's up to me what is forgivable and unforgivable
2728 I choose everything to be forgivable

2729 I believe in no statute of limitations on forgiveness
2730 It's okay to forgive someone over and over again
2731 Today I give forgiveness the time it needs to mature
2732 I forgive, regardless of whether I am forgiven by others
2733 One of my greatest abilities is my ability to forgive
2734 I accept the forgiveness of others

General Health Concerns

OUCH! Yeah, we all create body issues, don't we? How we respond to them determines if we will help heal ourselves, or hurt ourselves. Focusing on the gratitude you feel for your body is one step in the right direction. Saying positive affirmations about your body is another powerful step towards self-healing.

2735 I can easily digest all types of foods
2736 My body is, and will remain, cancer-free
2737 My body is, and will remain, disease-free
2738 With every breath I become healthier
2739 I remain healthy throughout my entire life
2740 It's okay to be zit-free
2741 I deserve to have smooth, wrinkle-free skin
2742 Any pains I've had, now disappear
2743 I remember to take my medication
2744 My sense of smell is keener each day
2745 I am free of migraines
2746 I am free from allergies
2747 I am free from any aches and pains
2748 I remain free from Alzheimer's
2749 I remain free from Osteoporosis
2750 I remain free from cancer
2751 I remain free from AIDS and HIV
2752 Diseases flee from my body
2753 My immune system strengthens daily
2754 I am free from any heart diseases
2755 I release any and all cholesterol problems
2756 My cholesterol level is at a perfect number
2757 I release my diabetes to the Universe
2758 I possess a healthy outlook on life
2759 Remembering to thank my organs brings me joy
2760 My joints are moving easier each day
2761 Any ailments I've had I release in this moment

2762   I release from my Being any signs of allergies
2763   My cell structure changes for the better daily
2764   I enjoy perfect health throughout my life
2765   I feel completely healthy today
2766   I release any residue of a headache
2767   My head feels clear and pain-free
2768   I am free from any physical discomfort
2769   I'm now free from any kind of headaches
2770   Migraines are part of my past that I release now
2771   My eyesight returning to 20/20 is becoming a reality
2772   Any throat problems I've had are cleared up now
2773   I am free from suffering from heartburn
2774   I relax my body and migraines quickly go away
2775   I easily meditate away any migraine symptoms
2776   My stomach acids are always normal
2777   My stomach remains calm today
2778   The iron in my blood is now at a perfect level
2779   Every moment I become saner
2780   I easily release insanity from my mind
2781   My body responds well to medication
2782   My digestive system works perfectly at all times
2783   My elimination system works perfectly at all times
2784   I'm now free from manic-depression
2785   Tension headaches are part of my past
2786   I digest all food quickly and easily
2787   I'm free from all health problems today
2788   I relinquish the desire to use illness to get attention
2789   I'm now free from carpal tunnel and its symptoms
2790   It's okay to pamper myself when I'm sick
2791   It's okay to pamper myself when I'm well
2792   I focus on my health and how good I feel
2793   I'm finished with focusing on my illness
2794   My tension headache is disappearing; bye headache
2795   I know everything is curable
2796   My blood pressure is now returning to normal
2797   I've now chosen to outgrow my allergies

2798 I choose to be free from stuttering
2799 My body is now producing fewer gasses
2800 I'm now free from a condition called insomnia
2801 I'm now free from any kind of phobias
2802 I'm now free from carpal tunnel
2803 I'm now free from fibromyalgia
2804 I'm now free from Hepatitis
2805 I choose to end any internal wars and battles now
2806 My physical state is improving daily
2807 I ignore my doctor's death sentence and live
2808 I live healthily and joyfully my entire life

General Skills to Improve

Did you know I type 128 wpm? It's true. I'm a freak in that way. Does it make me better than you? No way. I'm sure you do things better than me in lots of other areas. We all have things we do well in life, and other areas we'd like to improve. Take time to do a few affirmations from this section and begin to focus on what skills you'd like to improve.

2809 Every day I'm getting better at math
2810 Every day I'm easily able to spell with more accuracy
2811 Every day I move with more pride and confidence
2812 I choose to be more intelligent, and so it is
2813 My vocabulary increases rapidly and easily
2814 My typing speed is increasing every day
2815 I balance my checkbook quickly and accurately
2816 I'm becoming more physically coordinated every day
2817 My handwriting is becoming more legible every day
2818 I'm more graceful in all of my movements now
2819 I'm getting better and better at public speaking
2820 I remember jokes and relay them well
2821 I'm getting better at figuring out how to fix my hair
2822 Putting make-up on is now a skill that I do well
2823 I remember to breathe as I did when I was a baby
2824 I'm learning how to sew, and getting better every day
2825 I can learn anything I set my mind to
2826 Every day my art skills improve
2827 I'm a wonderful singer, and I do it with gusto
2828 I'm qualified to be an excellent driver
2829 Cooking is a form of relaxation and I enjoy it
2830 Every day I become a better cook
2831 My reading speed and comprehension increase
2832 My grammar improves daily
2833 I resolve now to spend more time at the library
2834 I'm becoming a better swimmer every day

2835 I'm good at putting things together
2836 I can repair household items quickly and easily
2837 I'm finding learning new languages easy and fun
2838 I'm doing well learning how to play an instrument
2839 I thank God that I can read and write
2840 I know today I'm capable of fixing anything

Goals

It's amazing how many people are vague about what they really want in life. Ask some people what they want and you'll usually hear what they don't want. Is it any wonder they're not getting spectacular experiences? Begin by figuring out something you really truly wish to achieve, and then begin to do affirmations and focus on it until it arrives. It's closer than you think!

2841 My goals are becoming manifest
2842 There is plenty of time to accomplish my goals
2843 I use all the tools God has given me to reach my goals
2844 Accomplishment of my goals is part of my reality
2845 I commit myself to my goals
2846 It's logical for me to believe I can achieve my goals
2847 God knows my goals and helps me to achieve them
2848 I lay aside old goals and replace them with new goals
2849 My major goal is to show the Universe my true essence
2850 My goals go along well with my destiny
2851 The goal to survive is a good goal
2852 Onc goal today is to make it through the day
2853 I choose to live to see my children respect my views
2854 Goal setting becomes easier for me every day
2855 I set goals that challenge me and that I happily achieve
2856 I enjoy being focused on my goals, and on the moment
2857 It's time to reach for the goals I've set for myself
2858 My goals and motivation make a great combination
2859 I have the necessary passion to accomplish my goals
2860 My goals are clearer to my consciousness every day
2861 I enjoy making reachable goals; all goals are reachable
2862 I keep my eye on my goals and ignore obstacles
2863 I have a deep inner knowing that I'll reach all my goals
2864 I am totally committed to the completion of my goals
2865 I commit myself to my goal, and things begin to happen

Good Fortune

Some believe in good luck, others in good fortune. If you are one who wishes to focus on good fortune, this short section is for you.

2866 It's time for me to accept my good fortune
2867 I'm very fortunate in all areas of my life
2868 I'm free from guilt about my increased good fortune
2869 I deserve to continue having good fortune
2870 My good fortune is here to stay
2871 I accept good fortune now
2872 I'm ready for my good fortune
2873 Today I find good fortune everywhere I go
2874 My good fortune has a way of catching up to me
2875 I continue to have good luck and good fortune
2876 Good fortune shines on me today and every day
2877 Today I allow my good fortune to materialize
2878 Today I prove one can be positive and rich

Grief

This is a potentially tough section, and yet also a section of great healing. We've all felt, or will all feel, grief. It doesn't have to be from deaths, it can be from job losses, love losses, even the loss of youth. Grief usually entails something you wish you had, but no longer (or will never) have. However, it is a temporary state of being. It does not define you. Embrace grief. Hold it in your arms and thank it for the human experience of grief that we all share. Then it's time to do some affirmations to allow it to move on and to return to joy.

2879 God showers healing upon me in these times
2880 I forgive anyone close to me who has died
2881 Mourning is a part of life and I'm surviving
2882 I'm willing to get on with my life
2883 I'm now discovering new strengths in myself
2884 I give my grief over to God now and always
2885 It's okay to take time to grieve
2886 I pamper myself while I heal
2887 It's okay to be angry at having to grieve
2888 I'm through grieving and move onto other emotions
2889 It's possible to intersperse happiness in grief
2890 I choose to be happy today
2891 Grieving is tiring; I ask for, and receive extra energy
2892 I get lots of rest during these times, as I need it
2893 I'm hanging in there, which is okay for now
2894 It's okay to feel overwhelmed and hide under the covers
2895 It's okay to forget about life before the loss
2896 I remember what my life was like before the loss
2897 I choose to feel my loved one's presence today
2898 I wrap myself up in God's healing arms today
2899 Grief lives in the past; the present holds only peace
2900 I relinquish this overwhelming sense of grief and loss

2901 Grieving takes time; I give it the time it needs
2902 I feel the angels holding me as I grieve today
2903 My tears are cleansing and it's okay to shed them
2904 I continue to look for the rainbows after storms
2905 I place a high price on my mental sanity today
2906 I give myself a break today
2907 I relax and let all the feelings come out today
2908 When people ask me how I feel, I can handle it
2909 I feel the strength hidden inside the weakness
2910 I'm able to give a spiritual hug to my loved one today
2911 Emotionally and physically I'm stronger today
2912 I feel the spirits who are helping me with grieving
2913 Grief takes on many forms and I accept God's help
2914 I easily experience closure when events in my life end
2915 I deserve to take special time for myself now
2916 It's okay to grieve for the way things used to be
2917 It's okay to grieve for all perceived losses
2918 It's okay to heal my grief today

Healing of the Planet

How we focus on our world helps to create it. It may seem an overwhelming and awesome job, but it's truly an awesome opportunity to contribute something good. Use this section to focus on healing your environment and planet and feel the love coming back to you.

2919 We are all on the same side, which I remember now
2920 There is enough food for everyone to eat
2921 There is space on the planet for everyone to live richly
2922 Today I show the world the light in me
2923 I'm proud to be part of a community of loving souls
2924 I pray for fewer and fewer global accidents today
2925 I pray for less and less global anger today
2926 I enjoy being a part of my world
2927 I have faith in the future of the world
2928 I'm dedicated to the cause of world peace
2929 I pray for increased good-will between countries
2930 I have faith in the goodness of mankind
2931 I choose to notice the good in people today
2932 I choose to see a kind and loving world around me
2933 I consciously give love and positive energy to the world
2934 I choose to see my brothers and sisters as equal
2935 My world is a place of beauty
2936 I help humanity one heart at a time
2937 I'm committed to making the world a better place
2938 I extend my essence of love and joy to the planet
2939 I join with my sisters and brothers to save the world
2940 My part in saving the world is an important one
2941 There is much good in the world and I accept it
2942 My honest opinion is useful to the planet
2943 How I perceive the world is up to me
2944 I love taking care of my environment
2945 I have faith in the goodness of others
2946 I remember to recycle

2947 Recycling has become an easy habit for me
2948 I care about the future of the planet
2949 My contributions to the planet are vital for its success
2950 My environment and I get along very well
2951 Cleaning up the planet is part of my job on Earth
2952 I join the world in a prayer to repair the ozone layer
2953 I remember to send energy and peace to others today
2954 This is the year we overcome the homeless challenge
2955 Today I send energy, hope and love to the homeless
2956 When I hear a siren, I pray for everyone involved
2957 The sun, moon, stars and planets are my friends
2958 Life has abundance of love, trust and compassion
2959 I trust the ultimate goodness of humanity
2960 I join the world in praying for a cure for AIDS
2961 I see the world extending love to people with HIV/AIDS
2962 I love all my fellow humans
2963 I am on the side for peace
2964 Since I know hate breeds hate, I send love to prisoners
2965 I join the world in saying a prayer for true world peace
2966 I join the world in saying a prayer for world prosperity
2967 Being a part of the solution is fun and exciting for me
2968 There is something I can do to help the world situation
2969 This country is well on its way to repairing past mistakes
2970 The economy in my world is improving daily
2971 Visualizing world peace is an act I perform daily
2972 I visualize my love and energy extending to the world
2973 Any work for peace and goodness is worthwhile
2974 I have a loving community that supports me
2975 I send love from my heart, sweeping over the planet
2976 The time has come for world peace and I'm helping
2977 Today I pray for children everywhere
2978 The love I feel for humanity is catching
2979 I wish abundance onto all of humanity
2980 I send love, energy and peace to everyone
2981 The planet needs my help and I give it now
2982 I support and trust my local police officers

2983 Today my neighborhood remains free from violence
2984 I send love to storms to diffuse their power
2985 I hold great respect for farmers and their families
2986 My love is helping to heal the world
2987 I support all those who are working for peace and love
2988 I pray today for all who are endangered species
2989 I send love to all my foreign brothers and sisters
2990 I help clean up my environment each day
2991 The hope I have for the future of the world is contagious
2992 I pray for all people considering ending their own life
2993 I pray for all people considering ending another life
2994 I send love and healing to racial hate groups today
2995 I continue to bond with the human race
2996 The world and I are constantly evolving
2997 My faith in people grows each day
2998 The beauty of the world reveals itself to me
2999 I treat street people with love and respect
3000 I join the world in a prayer for those known as "bums"
3001 People are inherently good in my world
3002 I communicate with the stars, the planets and the air
3003 I communicate with the earth, and the water
3004 My world is now free from wars
3005 The whole world is rising up to its potential, and so am I
3006 This disease called AIDS is now being globally cured
3007 My eyes reflect the love I feel toward humanity today
3008 My heart is full of unconditional love towards all
3009 I choose to connect with humanity today
3010 Through my eyes I see a beautiful world
3011 Competition no longer exists in my world
3012 I reconsider my views on the death penalty
3013 I reconsider my views on hating those who hate
3014 I send waves of love through the atmosphere
3015 It's time for me to pay attention to my environment
3016 I have a responsibility to humanity to stay peaceful
3017 I contribute to the positive changes of the world
3018 I'm now co-creating a world of equality

3019 I choose to bolster the peace movement today
3020 I help stop the creation of new diseases
3021 I see the beauty in people and in my environment
3022 My world has a new, powerful, loving understanding
3023 Positive thoughts in the world form a synthesis today
3024 I choose to trust my fellow humans more each day
3025 It takes only a moment to alter the energy of the world
3026 I pray for all news events in the world
3027 I do my part to heal the world today
3028 I send my earth home nurturing love and healing today
3029 I share the best of myself with the world today
3030 My mind firmly holds onto the idea of world peace
3031 Let's all join together and give the world a healing kiss
3032 I choose to pray today for the hearts of terrorists
3033 I choose to believe in a world of honest police officers
3034 All the police officers in my world are trustworthy
3035 I believe that advertisers are becoming more honest
3036 Today I choose to pray for the condition called acid rain
3037 Today I pray for the condition called global warming
3038 I now create the environment in which I wish to live
3039 I can create anything in my earthly environment
3040 I'm now living in an enlightened society
3041 My love is having a sweeping effect over this country
3042 Teachers are some of our biggest assets
3043 In this moment, there are cures for all diseases
3044 I choose to believe in Earth day everyday
3045 I live in a world where we are all committed to love
3046 I send love to all who prostitute their bodies
3047 I send love to all who feel they must prostitute integrity
3048 Today I choose to live in a crime-free neighborhood

Healing

While you're busy sending healing thoughts to the planet, take a few moments to focus some of that healing upon yourself. FEEL the healing energy going into each cell and purifying and cleansing it.

3049 I accept healing energy from the Universe
3050 I accept God's healing for me and my family today
3051 Revealing my past to the world is okay and healing
3052 It's acceptable and healing to nurture myself
3053 I deserve to be healed
3054 It's okay to be radically and miraculously healed
3055 In this moment, I recover to my former good health
3056 I believe in miracles, beyond all doubt
3057 It's okay to give myself time to heal properly
3058 I choose to heal my childhood dramas today
3059 Old mental scars are now healed within my mind
3060 I believe in, deserve and anticipate my healing now
3061 I choose alternative healing today in place of medication
3062 I choose to let my wounds be healed today
3063 I locate the point of my pain and visually remove it
3064 I visualize my arthritis crumbling into dust today
3065 I see clear, pure liquid flushing toxins from my body
3066 I am my own best emotional healer

Holidays / Birthdays

Holidays and birthdays are often filled with joy. Sometimes they're also filled with... odd experiences which pop up to test us. Take a few moments to read these and feel if any of them apply to you.

3067 I enjoy getting a year older
3068 I remain cheerful during all holidays
3069 This birthday all my wishes come true
3070 I enjoy having birthdays
3071 I celebrate my birthday giving to others
3072 As birthdays come and go, I remain young
3073 I spend a portion of my birthday in quiet reflection
3074 I have done a good job so far with my life
3075 Christmas is a time to communicate with my Creator
3076 It's a good time to communicate with my Creator
3077 I enjoy all facets of the Christmas season
3078 I love to celebrate Kwanza with my loved ones
3079 I enjoy the Hanukkah season and the love it brings
3080 I find perfect gifts for all the people on my giving list
3081 This holiday, I take time to enjoy the season
3082 During the holiday season, I have plenty of time for me
3083 I remain calm and joyful during all holiday gatherings
3084 I'm now free from worrying about holidays
3085 The day I was born is a day I always enjoy
3086 I was born at exactly the right time in history
3087 It's okay to get birthday wishes and presents
3088 I remember birth dates of all my friends/family/relatives
3089 This holiday I choose to help those less fortunate
3090 I start the New Year sending peace and love

Homeowner Challenges

Yea, we're homeowners! Ohhhh noooo, that means we're responsible for everything!   Sound familiar? Keep your focus and your expectations of your home positive and you'll form a beautiful partnership together. Wanting to sell your home? There are some affirmations for you in here as well.

3091 I take care of all home improvements beautifully
3092 My pipes always remain in perfect working order
3093 It's fun to paint my house when it needs it
3094 My house and I are forming a new, close bond
3095 My home shelters me from the cold, and I thank it today
3096 It's great to have a place of love to come home to
3097 I'm now free forever from having to pay rent
3098 It's easy for me to find the perfect home for my needs
3099 I now find the home I can easily afford
3100 I now have a real estate agent that I trust
3101 I now have the money needed for my closing costs
3102 I have a real estate agent who looks out for my interests
3103 I now sell my house for the full asking price
3104 I make any placc I live feel like home
3105 I see my open house going smoothly
3106 Interest rates continually drop reaching a good number
3107 The offer I make is instantly accepted
3108 Moving to my new house goes very smoothly
3109 The house I'm buying is in very good shape
3110 Our house sells quickly and easily now
3111 Now is the time for our home to sell to its new owner
3112 I allow the Universe's help in the selling of our home
3113 With each breath, I have more faith in selling our home
3114 The new owners of our home are finding us now
3115 Our energies extend to those who love our home
3116 We have the perfect person to help us sell our home
3117 We now have the perfect way to sell our home

3118 Our home is now selling quicker than we expected
3119 The timing of the selling and buying works out perfectly
3120 God orchestrates the perfect timing of our home sale
3121 I relax and know that our house is selling
3122 Our house is now extending a beam of light to others
3123 We have lots of people who want to buy our home
3124 We receive offers above our asking price now
3125 It's amazing the good price we got for our house
3126 We are joyful as we sign the papers for our home sale
3127 We thank our home for the good years we've been here
3128 We ask our home to release us to our new home
3129 The entire home process goes exceedingly well
3130 I send love to all my major appliances
3131 I deserve the perfect house for my wants and needs
3132 I see myself easily making my house payments
3133 I make all decisions with confidence
3134 Keeping my house in tip top shape is part of the fun
3135 I bless my home and it blesses me
3136 I respect my home and the energies it contains
3137 My home always keeps us safe and loved
3138 I'm grateful for our home and treat it with love

Hopes and Dreams

This is a perfect time to focus on your hopes and dreams and bring them into reality! Don't wait for someone else to do it for you. Only you can bring your dreams to fruition.

3139 I'm now able to turn my dreams into realities
3140 It's okay to make my dreams come true
3141 I am guilt-free about making my dreams come true
3142 I own my dreams and I give them wings
3143 I'm dedicated to making my dreams my reality
3144 Watching my dreams become reality is exciting for me
3145 It's okay to have fun fulfilling my dreams
3146 The sooner I start my dream, the sooner it manifests
3147 I know dreams definitely come true
3148 All my dreams are destined to come true
3149 I let my wildest dreams come true
3150 I'm completely motivated to let my dreams come true
3151 I now refuse to give up my dreams
3152 It's okay to live my dream
3153 I choose today to begin to materialize my dream
3154 Today I confidently stride toward my dreams
3155 Fantasy is only reality that hasn't happened yet
3156 I visualize my dreams and bring them into being
3157 I manifest my desires quickly and joyfully

Hospital Stays / Doctor Visits

My apologies to doctors and health care professionals everywhere, but I know a lot of us do not feel calm when in your presence. With a bit of positive self-talk, you can make any hospital or doctor visits calmer and more helpful.

3158 Doctors are my friends
3159 My doctors and nurses always treat me with respect
3160 My hospital stay is very short and sweet
3161 My insurance covers every part of my hospital stay
3162 My insurance covers every part of my doctor visit
3163 My insurance covers every part of my prescriptions
3164 I like and respect the doctors in my insurance plan
3165 Visiting my doctor is a pleasurable experience for me
3166 I'm free from seeing my doctor as a God
3167 I now need doctors less and less
3168 The money I pay my doctor is always reasonable
3169 My doctor bills are always well within my means
3170 This hospital is well staffed
3171 I find the perfect doctor for my needs
3172 My stay in the hospital is pleasant and quick
3173 All my nurses treat me very well
3174 Doctors in this hospital have my best interests at heart
3175 It's okay to need therapy and counseling
3176 My therapist understands and helps me
3177 Needing mental help is okay
3178 I'm free from being ashamed of getting mental help
3179 It's all right to choose to have plastic surgery
3180 I leave this hospital even better than when I came in

Infertility

I have several friends who have dealt with this issue. One friend got Reiki treatments and did affirmations, and a year later cleared her energy and became pregnant. Don't give up the hope. Remember…focus on what you WANT, not on what you don't.

3181 Every day my ability to conceive children increases
3182 All of my bodily organs are functioning perfectly
3183 My body now grants my request to conceive
3184 My body continues to become more fertile every day
3185 All questions I have about infertility are easily answered
3186 The adoption process goes smoothly
3187 I make the right decisions for me
3188 I have many options and I choose them carefully now
3189 Answers to all my questions are given to me by God
3190 I allow the stress in my life to recede
3191 I have the ability to be a terrific parent
3192 Conceiving a child brings me great joy
3193 I deserve to be a parent
3194 I deserve to conceive a child
3195 My doctors and I work well together
3196 My partner remains understanding through this process
3197 I can easily afford fertility treatments
3198 Infertility is a word I've eliminated from my vocabulary
3199 Infertility is in my past and I release it now
3200 I accept the miracle of birth for myself
3201 I believe in myself and know I'll successfully conceive
3202 I deserve to hear the pitter-patter of my baby's feet

Landlords / Neighbors

I've moved a lot in my life, especially as a single mother. I've had times when I've loved my landlords and times when I most certainly didn't. Sending love to, and expecting the best of, your landlord and neighbors makes for much better relationships for all.

3203 My landlord and I think alike
3204 I'm able to communicate with my landlord very well
3205 I stay calm when speaking to my landlord
3206 My landlord is me in another form
3207 There is a beautiful spirit within my landlord
3208 I enjoy visiting with my landlord
3209 My landlord and I easily solve any disagreements
3210 I always get along with my neighbors
3211 My neighbors and I share many good times
3212 I feel good about the way I treat my neighbors
3213 How I treat my neighbors is the way they treat me
3214 I'm glad to have friendly, happy neighbors
3215 It's okay to trust my neighbors
3216 I deserve to have wonderful neighbors
3217 My neighborhood is filled with kind, generous people
3218 I deserve to have wonderful landlords
3219 When my neighbors succeed, I succeed
3220 I'm invited to all neighborhood functions
3221 I choose to love my neighbors
3222 I feel safe in my neighborhood now

Learning / College

We never stop learning. Some learn through colleges and other formal training, and all of us learn from everyday life. Focusing on what you want to achieve, combined with affirmation usage, will help you to reach your education goals.

3223 I get good grades in any classes I take
3224 My study habits improve daily
3225 I'm proud to be working towards a degree
3226 Going to college is a dream I'm making a reality
3227 I enjoy studying and learning
3228 I'm always well prepared for every test
3229 I'm now free of nightmares associated with school
3230 Studying is now easy for me and I do it well
3231 I'm able to study and learn under any circumstance
3232 I choose today to make a new friend to study with
3233 I love to learn and it comes easily to me
3234 My time spent studying is time well spent
3235 I arrive on time for all my classes today and always
3236 School is an exciting, important part of my life
3237 I'm thrilled with the opportunity to be a college student
3238 Realizing I'm fortunate, I make the most of college
3239 It's easy for me to choose my major, and I do it quickly
3240 I take classes right for my major and make great grades
3241 I have people helping me through my college years
3242 My living arrangements suit me perfectly
3243 I always have enough money for everything I need
3244 I get along well with my teachers
3245 I learn quickly and joyfully all throughout my lifetime
3246 I remember to learn something new each day

Legal Complications

This is another one of those times when our emotions can seem to take over. Staying focused on your desired outcomes, and remaining calm and loving helps the entire process. Remember to send extra positive energy to others around you, to help them in this area as well.

3247 Legally I'm very secure
3248 I release any and all legal complications to the Universe
3249 Whenever I need them, I have great attorneys
3250 There's always an attorney that meets my needs
3251 I decide what to do with legal issues
3252 It's ultimately my decision whether I want to go to court
3253 My day in court goes very well
3254 Today I convince the judge/jury of my innocence
3255 My wish to be free of any legal complications is granted
3256 I relinquish legal complications from my life
3257 It's okay to refrain from ever having to be in court
3258 When chosen for a jury, I handle my job well
3259 I enjoy being part of a jury, and I do it well
3260 I believe the legal system is becoming fairer for all
3261 I send love to anyone involved in legal complications
3262 I trust my lawyer completely and my lawyer trusts me
3263 I raise my consciousness when it comes to lawyers
3264 Lawyers are my friends
3265 My guardian angel and my lawyer's speak frequently
3266 All of my legal matters are only temporary

Loss of Job / Looking for Work

Here is an area which can be potentially filled with
excitement. What's more exciting than the prospect of
finding a new job doing something you LOVE and
getting paid generously for it? What? That hasn't been
your experience?   If you're looking for work, spend a bit
of time here first. Raising your vibration (and your
expectations) and visualizing a positive outcome, will
get you the jobs you love and the high pay you deserve.

3267 Today I find the most fabulous job of my life
3268 I now visualize myself in the perfect job for me
3269 It's okay to be out of a job
3270 I am a wonderful person regardless of my job status
3271 When looking for work, God provides me with strength
3272 I choose to find work quickly
3273 It's okay to find my perfect job, quickly and easily
3274 The first impression I give is always a positive one
3275 The last impression I give is always a positive one
3276 The time I take to job hunt is time well spent
3277 Yes, I do have the energy and desire to job hunt today
3278 Every career move I make turns out to be a positive one
3279 I'm filled with positive vibes about today's interview
3280 My interviewer is nervous too; I send us both peace
3281 I feel secure in the new job that I've just received
3282 I choose to be well liked and respected in my new job
3283 I fearlessly speak my views when leaving my job
3284 It's okay to burn bridges; God builds new ones
3285 My career is right on track
3286 I let God pick my job for me now
3287 My working hours fit in perfectly with my lifestyle
3288 The amount of hours I work is exactly what I want now
3289 I'm proud of the way I get up after being knocked down
3290 I take a deep breath, and find a new job today
3291 I deserve to find the perfect job for me

3292 I am worthy of obtaining employment
3293 The interviewing process is what I do well
3294 I make favorable impressions when interviewing
3295 When it comes to employment I know what I want
3296 I have all the qualifications I need to pursue my career
3297 Career decisions are best made by God and me
3298 The world always provides a job for me
3299 I'm highly employable
3300 I go into each interview well prepared
3301 My positive energy shines through during my interview
3302 All my auditions go very well today
3303 God has found the perfect job for me and I accept it
3304 It's okay to be fired
3305 Even good people get fired
3306 It's easy for me to find the job that I love
3307 I easily ask for the salary I desire and I get it
3308 I make the perfect amount of money

Love

What is there to say about love? It's not just an emotion; it's a state of being. Love is not wimpy or weak. Love is the strongest energy there is. Tap into some of this strong, loving energy today, and remember to share it with others along the way. Remember, the more you love yourself, the more love you have for others; so, choose to uplift yourself with self-love today!

3309 It's always the perfect time and place for love
3310 I extend love easily and regularly
3311 I bask in the love from humanity
3312 I am joyful and loving for now and forever
3313 My heart overflows with love and acceptance
3314 Love is my powerful friend
3315 I am thankful for love and acceptance on all levels
3316 Today I commit myself to spreading love
3317 I remember to tell my family "I love you"
3318 I remember to tell my partner "I love you"
3319 I enjoy giving and receiving love
3320 I love what I am
3321 I love the way I act
3322 I love and accept all of me
3323 There is a never-ending flow of love around me
3324 I move gracefully in the world today
3325 I feel love being extended
3326 I accept all displays of love today
3327 It's possible to be confident and loving, and I am
3328 Today I choose to speak lovingly to everyone
3329 My love for life is apparent today
3330 I'm very affectionate and loving
3331 I love myself, always and completely
3332 I love what I've become
3333 I love what I haven't become
3334 I love myself for treating others well

3335 I love myself for treating myself well
3336 Loving myself is easy for me now
3337 Loving myself means I'm able to love others more
3338 Deciding to love myself is a good decision
3339 I let my love for myself increase each day
3340 My self-esteem grows in proportion to my self-love
3341 My attitude about loving myself is contagious
3342 When I extend love, others notice my radiance
3343 I always live with myself, so I have healthy self-love
3344 The more I love myself, the better my overall health
3345 I mentally and physically caress and cuddle myself
3346 I relax into the process of mastering self-love
3347 I always come from a loving place when I speak
3348 Today I start loving myself more
3349 I believe it when people tell me they love me
3350 It's okay to publicly show affection and love
3351 I deserve to be loved for who I am
3352 I love every aspect of the life I've been given
3353 I express my views clearly and with love today
3354 I choose to love the place in which I live
3355 I send love and success thoughts to my competitors
3356 I believe I'm very lovable
3357 I now am more loving to all my so-called enemies
3358 I take hatred and I turn it into love
3359 Waves of love wash over me today
3360 It's heartwarming to know people love and support me
3361 I easily express my feelings of love today
3362 I'm very much in love with life
3363 My greatest improvement is my extending of love
3364 I send love to the elderly in this moment
3365 I treat the elderly with respect and love
3366 The love I send out today stems from my energy source
3367 I am in a constant state of love
3368 My heart has the ability to ceaselessly send forth love
3369 My overwhelming motivation is love
3370 I have the means to love the entire world

3371 I am here to love
3372 My heart opens up to receive all love
3373 I feel an abundance of love and send it back out
3374 My love flows to all who need love
3375 I deserve to be treated with love, respect and kindness
3376 I choose to believe in the power of love
3377 I apply love generously to each situation today
3378 When I allow it to be, love is always enough
3379 I know people want love, and I give it willingly
3380 I walk softly and carry only love
3381 I live in a world filled with loving, caring people
3382 My inner child receives my love today
3383 It's okay to feel loved
3384 I am very loving
3385 I love humankind
3386 I love spiritkind
3387 I love myself unconditionally
3388 I love others unconditionally
3389 Loving myself comes naturally to me
3390 I stand for love
3391 My love is free from being circumstance-dependent
3392 Loving humanity feels natural and familiar
3393 Today I choose to love more
3394 I do for others as it expresses my love
3395 When I extend love, I receive love
3396 I'm able to continue to love myself
3397 I remember to be loving today
3398 I love who I'm becoming
3399 I love my life and all who are a part of it
3400 I am 100% pure love
3401 I love every facet of my life
3402 I love every facet of my existence
3403 My attitude today reflects the love within me
3404 My time loving others is well spent
3405 I bask in the feelings of peace and love
3406 I accept love from others

3407 I have complete, unconditional love within me
3408 Everyone I see today needs love and acceptance
3409 The people in my life all realize how much I love them
3410 When there's a retaliation method, I choose love
3411 Finding the love in others is on my agenda today
3412 I love every part of what makes me what I am
3413 I am love incarnate
3414 It's okay to expect and receive love and support
3415 I learn more about what love means today
3416 Today wherever I perceive hate, I shower it with love
3417 I'm very devoted to promoting my own position of love
3418 Love is becoming more predominant in our culture
3419 Today I identify another person's need for love
3420 I give love freely today
3421 I choose to perform acts of love and kindness today

Luck

I've been told I'm very lucky. One of my main hobbies is entering sweepstakes online. I've written a book entitled "Ready, Click, Win!" which shows others how to do this fun, easy and lucrative hobby.   I've won hundreds of things over the years and it's always been a lot of fun. I talk with people a lot about how to enter sweeps, and I love it when others win as well.

 What I find most often, from those who do not win, is the negative way they talk to themselves. They will actually write me and say: "I never win anything", "if it weren't for bad luck, I'd have none at all".   Not a huge shock to me why they're not winning, how about to you? You make your own luck, and believing you can win and focusing on your luck is a huge step in the process of bringing fun wins to you of all kinds. Remember to stay loving and generous in the process, for stingy thoughts only bring stingy wins. Have fun with this one and see if your luck begins to improve.

3422 I make my own good luck
3423 I'm a very lucky person
3424 I am entering a very long lucky time of my life
3425 Good luck is everywhere
3426 I feel lucky today
3427 I'm guilt-free about being lucky
3428 Lucky times are here
3429 I feel lucky to know all the people I have in my life
3430 I accept all good luck that comes my way today
3431 My luck now changes to the good, forever
3432 I have a feeling that my luck is changing for the better
3433 I help my good luck along with positive actions
3434 I make my own good luck
3435 My good luck is now coming to pass

Men

What an odd section title. "Men"? Don't worry, there's one entitled "Women" as well. Women have issues with men and vice versa and it's not helpful to focus on old stereotypes of either sex. We also sometimes have trouble with our own sex. Take this time to feel if any of these thoughts are ones you now choose to use.

3436 I always use my chosen birth control method
3437 I still feel like a man when doing the dishes
3438 I don't claim to understand my wife, I just love her
3439 My courtship with my wife continues our entire lives
3440 Males are magnificent
3441 Females and males are equal in truth
3442 I'm proud to be a man
3443 My masculinity is part of me
3444 I'm free of any male stigmas
3445 I'm a prince
3446 I'm the most handsome man in the Universe
3447 I'm aging very well
3448 I have many male and female friends
3449 I remain free of prostate cancer my entire life
3450 My girlfriend is a remarkable woman
3451 Men of all shapes and sizes are handsome
3452 It's okay that I'm losing my hair
3453 I remain sexy when my head is balding
3454 There are plenty of good, honest women in this world
3455 I'm a very lucky man
3456 I'm a remarkable man
3457 My partner is a remarkable person
3458 I'm a man of my word
3459 My scalp continues to grow hair my entire life
3460 I'm free from feeling I have to act like a big boy
3461 I now have a wonderful woman in my life
3462 I have an equally high opinion of women and men

3463 I am free from female-bashing now and always
3464 I am free from male-bashing now and always

Metaphysical / New Age

Ah yes, one of my most favorite sections. For over 25 years I have been involved in metaphysical study (the word "metaphysical" simply means "beyond physical"). I hope you enjoy this next section and this focus.

3465 I have come well prepared for this life
3466 I deserve total peace and enlightenment
3467 I experience life on the earth plane to its fullest
3468 I'm easily able to release my attachment to conflicts
3469 Everything holds meaning, yet nothing holds meaning
3470 It's okay to let people's harsh words bounce off of me
3471 My fellow humans are my dear brothers and sisters
3472 There is a light in me
3473 The light inside me shines love and acceptance to all
3474 I deserve to remember who I am
3475 Today IS the rest of my life
3476 I'm thrilled to have the opportunity to experience Earth
3477 I consciously guide my energies
3478 Forever is a concept I'm beginning to fathom
3479 I understand why I'm here
3480 Great truths are revealed to my consciousness today
3481 I am now shown my limitlessness
3482 I own all of my experiences
3483 I am a miracle
3484 I consciously choose the treatment I will accept
3485 I absorb energy from my Source, constantly
3486 I trust myself to remember all that I'm here for
3487 I remember we are all one
3488 The time has come for me to change my reality
3489 Meditating helps me to make sound decisions
3490 I remember to meditate every day
3491 I deserve to find time in my day to meditate
3492 I choose to focus on my heart today
3493 I choose to set aside the ego in this moment

3494 I am calmly ignoring the ego
3495 I give away my power to me and only me
3496 The old me and the new me are friends
3497 My search for enlightenment is successful
3498 My expectations (of myself and others) are diminishing
3499 Let the world call me crazy, I know who I am
3500 Everyone I meet is me in another form
3501 So-called authority figures and I are equal in truth
3502 I lovingly release to the Universe attack thoughts
3503 The person I most want to be like... is myself
3504 The person I would most like to meet... is myself
3505 When I speak to someone I am speaking to myself
3506 I deserve to rid myself of limiting beliefs
3507 I choose out of high drama encounters today
3508 I choose what I feed my mind
3509 The goodness within me comes forth now
3510 My soul loves freedom
3511 I invite all friendly spirits to share my existence
3512 I relinquish my feelings of hopelessness
3513 I choose to follow divine guidance
3514 I'm who I need to be in this moment
3515 I am peacefully going beyond the limits of the ego
3516 I easily and regularly outtalk the ego
3517 I've given up all attack thoughts
3518 I remember to meditate regularly
3519 We are all equally divinely inspired
3520 My life's teachers are all around me
3521 I commit myself to my life
3522 I allow all good things to come to me today
3523 My likes and dislikes belong to me and are okay
3524 I feel I'm a part of something bigger than myself
3525 The time of making excuses for my actions is over
3526 It's okay to admit my psychic tendencies
3527 I am love
3528 My greatest wish is to be more myself
3529 Wherever I go, I meet beautiful spirits

3530 I remember I'm able to make conscious choices
3531 I'm able to see auras clearer every time I try
3532 Reading other people's energy is natural for me
3533 Reading my own energy is natural for me
3534 I'm able to center my energies very rapidly at will
3535 I listen to my inner voice
3536 I'm free from letting the ego taunt me
3537 I relinquish all violence from my consciousness
3538 I accept emotional and spiritual healing today
3539 I tap into my vast internal knowledge now
3540 I feel upbeat and refreshed after meditation
3541 I consult my inner self when making decisions
3542 My time on Earth is spent constructively and joyfully
3543 I own my own reality
3544 I am whole and complete
3545 I deserve to be free from limits
3546 I deserve to be free from judgments
3547 I am here for a great purpose
3548 Every breath in, is a choice for life
3549 With every breath I become more enlightened
3550 It's okay to speak my truth
3551 Everything is coming together for my highest good
3552 My past has served its purpose and I easily let it go
3553 I easily let my future be, and flow joyfully to me
3554 I live in the present and I easily let it be
3555 Every day I become freer of illusions
3556 Guidance is given to me constantly
3557 I receive guidance readily
3558 I easily make choices for my higher good
3559 I now feel worthy of accepting my inheritance
3560 I am an exquisite creator
3561 Saving myself is saving the world
3562 Today I choose to open up my mind's eyes
3563 I see others through my spiritual eyes
3564 Tomorrow is now and I choose to live in this moment
3565 Today I choose to be fully aware

3566 I'm here for the experience
3567 I choose to relax and tune into my inner voice
3568 I choose to transcend karmic law
3569 Insights are equal in truth
3570 I'm as important as Jesus, Buddha and other masters
3571 I choose present-moment awareness
3572 I'm free from the need to wear masks
3573 I'm here for sensational experiences
3574 I'm directly connected to my energy source
3575 Today I remember that I am pure consciousness
3576 It's okay to let any evil spirits leave my consciousness
3577 My time on planet Earth is precious and I treasure it
3578 My spirit's fountain of youth springs forth
3579 I allow my spirit to fly free today
3580 I gain strength from my spiritual energy source
3581 There is room in my mind for all that I choose to learn
3582 I see the totality of my Being today and always
3583 I am free from the concept that I am only a body
3584 Within the light there is understanding; I choose the light
3585 I pat the ego on the head and send it away today
3586 I invite the light
3587 Today I choose peace over any illusions
3588 At the center of my existence is love
3589 I have compassion for all as I am part of all
3590 I awaken to my true self today
3591 I choose to now easily detect the presence of angels
3592 Every day I discover new pathways in my mind
3593 I focus on my consciousness and am energized
3594 Enlightenment has reached my consciousness
3595 I have everlasting peace while I'm still in this body
3596 The angels and I work together to save the world
3597 My core Being seems deeply hidden, yet is right here
3598 I am free of the belief that I am fragmented from God
3599 I am part of the Oneness, and as such, I am everything
3600 I am instantly centered in this moment
3601 Take my desperation, Holy Spirit

3602 I choose to ignore insults and send the bearers love
3603 I play tag with my angels; I think it's my turn to "be it"
3604 Whatever happens, I remain centered
3605 Who I am is more important than what I do
3606 I transform the meaning I give to items in my life
3607 I choose carefully what I believe
3608 I choose to dissolve any insane thoughts that arise
3609 I enter very deeply into my own spirit now
3610 It's okay to make small steps toward enlightenment
3611 I'm liberated from feeling separated from my Creator
3612 My life is filled with miracles and revelations
3613 I am willing to be awakened from this dream
3614 I am responsible for what I do and what I think
3615 The memory of God is within each one of us
3616 I choose to continue to make conscious choices
3617 I choose to be filled with energy, love and light today
3618 I discover a bread crumb today
3619 I forgive myself for when I listen to the ego
3620 I forgive myself for being fooled by the ego
3621 I loosen my grip on having a desired outcome
3622 The nudge from my spirit guides feels natural
3623 I now tap into the knowledge I possess
3624 My time on Earth is precious and I treat it as such
3625 Activities take on a new flavor when I remain aware
3626 I now shift my perceptions towards joy and love
3627 I'm now comfortable following my bliss
3628 I easily and joyfully follow the urgings of my Inner Self
3629 My ultimate proof of love to the world is to be myself
3630 Seeing myself in others is uplifting and educational
3631 All people have chosen to be part of my consciousness
3632 I have the courage to feed my inner self instead of ego
3633 It's okay to have my own private sanctuary
3634 I surrender to my higher power now, in this moment
3635 My thoughts join with those of enlightened masters
3636 I take away the ego's power over me today
3637 I am my true self today

3638 I deserve to rub noses with my angels today
3639 I watch my thoughts as they float by today
3640 It's okay to experience psychic messages regularly
3641 Defending myself is a thing of the past for me
3642 I see my life change dramatically for the good
3643 Following advice from the ego seems silly now
3644   I release myself from ego's trap
3645 I now have the faith to believe in miracles
3646 I choose only the actions that are best for my higher self
3647 The angels applaud my transformation today
3648 I feel exhilarated when I give myself time to meditate
3649 I choose to let go of trying to make things happen today
3650 I choose to mentally align my chakras today
3651 Today I choose to spend time in awe of my Creator
3652 My spiritual routine is a time of tremendous joy for me
3653 My Inner Teacher shares my deepest desires
3654 I trust the voice of my own Inner Teacher
3655 When in doubt, I look inward
3656 I discover new insights about my thought processes
3657 It's okay to discover startling insights about myself now
3658 I discover the core of my being
3659 Today I choose to live my life by conscious choice
3660 All that matters is what I choose to do with this moment
3661 Today I choose to solve my problems using my soul
3662 I choose to be influenced only by my Inner Teacher
3663 I believe in the unlimitedness of the Self
3664 I am completely available to the present moment
3665 I trust the guidance my small Inner Voice reveals
3666 I now choose to believe pain is the illusion that it is
3667 I choose to realize I am awakening
3668 I'm done feeling anxious, and rejoice within the moment
3669 Bringing my thoughts to the present moment is a habit
3670 I feel centered and balanced now and remain this way
3671 I am only at the mercy of my thoughts about myself
3672 I take this current moment and alter it forever
3673 I change this current moment into one of joy

3674 True freedom is when I listen to my Inner Voice
3675 Today I choose to relinquish outward attachments
3676 Today I remember my true eternal home is Heaven
3677 Today I choose to exercise my telepathic powers
3678 I look beyond any human error to the divine within
3679 I choose to pay special attention to my inner child
3680 I choose to sing a duet with my inner child today
3681 I notice all the miracles that surround me today
3682 I let go of expectations
3683 I make room for joyful surprises
3684 I release my tight hold over outcomes today
3685 I'm in the presence of the Divine
3686 Miraculous things happen today
3687 I choose to breathe in the giggles of angels today
3688 I know a miracle when I see one, and I always see one
3689 I relinquish competitions with my sisters and brothers
3690 I let awareness change the mundane to miraculous

Minorities / Race Challenges

All people, of all colors, have those who do not wish well of them. It's a sad truth. It's been said that we put down that which we don't understand, so I hope one day we can all understand one another more and realize we are all part of the grand "oneness" of the Universe. This section is devoted to that vision.

3691 Racial slanders bounce off of me
3692 African Americans are my friends
3693 Caucasians are my friends
3694 Native Americans are my friends
3695 Polish Americans are my friends
3696 Mexican Americans are my friends
3697 Asian Americans are my friends
3698 Americans are my friends
3699 People of all races are my friends
3700 People of all countries are my friends
3701 All countries contain my brothers and sisters
3702 I choose to now be free of the term minority
3703 I find the color of my skin brings me great joy
3704 I see all of humanity through rose-colored glasses
3705 We are all the same; I remember that today
3706 Equality is color blind
3707 I believe the world is now freeing itself from racism
3708 We are all too smart to believe in, and support racism
3709 I choose to send love to all races and colors today
3710 Feelings of equality are spreading throughout the world
3711 I am an example of how to treat others as equals
3712 My decision to be racially color blind suits me
3713 I love my beautiful brown skin and I treat it with respect
3714 My olive complexion is beautiful and admired today
3715 I thank God that I have healthy, colorful skin
3716 I see in others only the bright light of their spirits
3717 Being part of a minority makes me feel special

3718 My status as a minority is only part of who I am
3719 The color of my skin is beautiful
3720 I love all of me, including the color of my skin
3721 My talents are far more than skin deep
3722 Discrimination tendencies are in my past and I let go
3723 Prejudice is a word that is now out of my vocabulary
3724 I choose to be free of all prejudices
3725 I've chosen to refrain from racial slander
3726 I make friends within all ethnic groups regularly
3727 I'm able to meet people from many different cultures
3728 I communicate well with people from different cultures

Money / Prosperity / Wealth

Cha-Ching! Who doesn't want more wealth? Okay, pretend you're all about just giving it to others. That's a good reason to get wealthy too. But don't feel guilty when you want to attract and accept more money for yourself. You deserve it.

3729 I deserve to be wealthy
3730 I deserve to make [insert dollar amount] per year
3731 I am wealthy
3732 I easily afford anything I choose to purchase
3733 I easily afford to pay all my bills
3734 I am calm and happy when paying my bills
3735 I remain calm every time I think of the bills I owe
3736 I calmly figure out ways to pay my bills
3737 I deserve money, to buy all the things I need and want
3738 I deserve to be a happy millionaire
3739 I deserve to remain a happy and calm millionaire
3740 It's okay to be rich when others are not
3741 There is plenty of money for me
3742 I deserve to have the energy of money
3743 Money Is innocent
3744 I choose to experience my great wealth
3745 It's okay to talk about money
3746 I enjoy finding money
3747 I remove any mental obstacles to my wealth
3748 I am self-sufficient, and I love it
3749 I'm through from having to get help with money again
3750 I am self-sufficient, starting NOW
3751 I enjoy going to the bank
3752 I receive checks in the mail on a regular basis
3753 I enjoy giving and receiving money
3754 I choose to change my ideas about money today
3755 I'm able to speak calmly with bill collectors
3756 Should creditors call, I gently explain my situation

3757 Bill collectors are people too
3758 I have enough self-worth today to talk to my creditors
3759 I claim my wealth and happiness
3760 I have decided to be wealthy
3761 Financial possibilities are all around me
3762 Financial stability is mine for the taking
3763 It's okay to be my age and be financially stable
3764 Financial success is now mine
3765 I deserve to have an exceptionally good credit rating
3766 I easily get any credit problems cleared up quickly
3767 Receiving bills is okay
3768 I trust myself to pay all my bills on time
3769 I am free from ever having to worry about money
3770 It's easy and fun to figure out my budget
3771 I stay within my budget very well
3772 I spend and live within my means
3773 I am now making [insert dollar amount] per month
3774 I am calmly enjoying being very wealthy
3775 I deserve to remain wealthy
3776 I deserve to enjoy being wealthy
3777 It's okay to be wealthy and happy
3778 It's okay to make more money than my parents
3779 It's okay to receive money from strangers
3780 It's okay to receive money from friends
3781 I bless and heal all my money situations
3782 I deserve great wealth
3783 There is enough money for everyone to be wealthy
3784 It's okay for me to receive my share of wealth
3785 It's okay to get unexpected money
3786 It's okay to receive money and to spend it on myself
3787 I can easily support myself
3788 I can easily support my family
3789 It's okay to accept money from my parents
3790 Saving money comes easily to me
3791 My ability to pay my bills reflects how I see myself
3792 I'm determined to increase my wealth today

3793 Changing my money habits comes easily to me
3794 I have fun organizing information for income taxes
3795 This year, my taxes are figured quickly and easily
3796 I enjoy the entire process of figuring my taxes
3797 I stay calm when preparing my income taxes this year
3798 I start my tax work sooner this year than last
3799 I'm free from ever having a tax audit
3800 I receive a lot of money back from the government
3801 I have my income taxes done by reliable accountants
3802 I feel in control of my tax preparations this year
3803 When preparing my taxes I'm calm and productive
3804 I'm immediately approved for bank loans
3805 I have excellent credit, and am approved for any loan
3806 Repaying my loans is easy for me
3807 I now visualize my bank account funds growing rapidly
3808 I visualize my wealth increasing today
3809 I learn quickly the best ways to invest my money
3810 My earnings are always increasing
3811 I'm able to save a good amount of money each month
3812 My savings accounts are increasing rapidly
3813 I'm balancing my checkbook better each month
3814 I'm now free from what is known as bouncing checks
3815 Whenever I need or desire money, it appears
3816 Today I choose to increase my wealth in all that I do
3817 My financial budget allows me to buy all that I want
3818 I easily pay off all my debts
3819 It's okay to be suddenly rich
3820 I'm financially able to give gifts to my friends and family
3821 There's a big possibility that I will be a millionaire
3822 It's okay to be rich and famous
3823 It's okay to want to have more money
3824 I now have an ever increasing annual income
3825 I now double my earnings each month
3826 I'm helping myself to my assets
3827 It's okay to be more financially secure than my friends
3828 I'm breaking the credit card habit

3829 It's okay to talk openly about money
3830 I deserve to wear expensive jewelry if I choose
3831 I deserve to wear designer clothing if I choose
3832 It's okay to accept gifts of money
3833 It's okay to be on financial assistance
3834 When necessary, it's okay to accept unemployment
3835 I make [insert desired number] dollars per hour
3836 My earnings increase with amazing rapidity
3837 Always having plenty of money is a luxury I now acquire
3838 I'm learning about purchasing stocks and do it very well
3839 My investments pay off at an alarmingly high rate
3840 I choose to do more than make ends meet now
3841 I'm comfortable receiving checks through the mail
3842 I can spend all my available cash, there's always more
3843 I have total control over my investments
3844 I have the ability to understand my finances
3845 Figuring my finances is now a joyful experience for me
3846 I'm now circulating money in a positive way
3847 I choose to be free of all debts from now on
3848 I choose to be free from poverty now and always
3849 I now love the rich, the poor and everything in between

New Day / Morning

Some people love to wake up early; some of us are night owls and go to bed when the sun rises. Use these affirmations in any way that suit you.

3850 I enjoy waking up early
3851 Whatever happens today, it remains a wonderful day
3852 Every morning that I wake up, I'm a better person
3853 I feel better when I get up early
3854 It's my choice, and I'm choosing to get out of bed
3855 I observe some silence in quiet preparation of my day
3856 I start this day with peace, joy and understanding
3857 I relax into my new day
3858 I expect, and have, a glorious day
3859 I expect good things to happen today, and they do
3860 I always immediately wake up joyful and refreshed
3861 I wake up on time easily without any alarm clock
3862 I enjoy waking up to a new day
3863 I look great even first thing in the morning
3864 I always awaken completely refreshed
3865 This day unfolds beautifully for me
3866 Today is an exceptionally good day
3867 I have a wonderful time today and it's a wonderful day
3868 My attitude determines the outcome of my day
3869 The minute the alarm rings I completely awaken
3870 Each day of my life is a new beginning
3871 It's a wonderful day and I'm anxious to get out of bed
3872 At any time during this day, I can begin the day anew
3873 I've decided to have a glorious day today
3874 I wake up early in the morning refreshed
3875 Today I choose to begin my day with inspiring thoughts
3876 I step into my day fearlessly, with faith and confidence
3877 I know I can make this day anything I choose
3878 This day is untouched by negativity, I keep it that way
3879 I set lots of small goals for myself today

Parents / Kids / Family

Is there a more highly charged subject than family? It's been said that we hurt the ones we love the most. It's time to change that. There is great joy to be found within each of your family relationships. You don't have to be and think and believe the same way as anyone else in your family. You can be unique and wonderful, just as you are. The more unconditional love you focus on your family, the more unconditional love you'll begin to receive back.

3880 Time spent with my children is fun
3881 It is possible to spend relaxing time with my children
3882 Raising happy, optimistic children is an important job
3883 However my children turn out, I know I've done my best
3884 My children are in God's hands, so I know they're safe
3885 My children are precious to me
3886 I easily sort out conflicting feelings about my parents
3887 I feel like a grown-up, even when around my parents
3888 My trust and support bring out the best in my children
3889 I give guidance to my kids with my words and actions
3890 My children are being influenced by my lifestyle
3891 I'm a good role model
3892 I'm taking the time to listen to my children
3893 I am learning when to keep silent
3894 I am a valuable teacher to my children
3895 I'm watching my child's body language
3896 I always perceive my children as precious to me
3897 My family is a source of continued joy
3898 I'm continually becoming closer to my Mom
3899 I'm continually becoming closer to my Dad
3900 Every day I understand my Mom more
3901 My family supports me in all I do
3902 I'm anticipating a fun visit with my parents
3903 It's okay to disagree with my parents

3904 It's easy for me to talk to my children about sex
3905 My children and I communicate well on all subjects
3906 I am unaffected by my children's whining
3907 I can believe differently than my parents
3908 I now free myself from my parents' opinion of me
3909 My parents think I'm a good person
3910 Regardless of how I act, I know my parents love me
3911 My parents' visits always seem short and sweet
3912 Our family sticks together through all times
3913 The respect I have for my parents remains constant
3914 My children always return safely to me
3915 I'm tender when dealing with my children
3916 I always make the right decisions with my children
3917 I include my children in some of the decision-making
3918 I teach my children the values I wish them to retain
3919 I decide against yelling at my children today
3920 My grandparents are important, and I visit them often
3921 When my children ask me questions, I'm always patient
3922 I remember to let my children speak their minds
3923 I set a good example for my children
3924 My kind words help to bring the family together
3925 My family eagerly shares household chores with me
3926 Asking my family to help around the house works well
3927 When dealing with my kids, I have a very long fuse
3928 I always know the most loving way to reprimand my kids
3929 My love for my children helps them in all things
3930 I'm able to afford instructional classes for my children
3931 I enjoy helping my children with their homework
3932 I'm smart enough to help my children with homework
3933 I have beautiful, healthy, happy children
3934 I easily discuss sex and birth control with my children
3935 I communicate well with my children's teachers
3936 I always take good care of my children
3937 I teach my children with patience and love
3938 I'm mature enough to be a good parent
3939 I have patience with my kids no matter what

3940 I let my children work through their problems today
3941 I understand what my children are going through
3942 I feel what my children are feeling today
3943 I'm always available for my children when they need me
3944 Deep inside I know my parents love me
3945 Deep inside I know my children love me
3946 I keep in close contact with my relatives
3947 My family accepts me as I am
3948 My friends accept me as I am
3949 I'm continually loved by my family
3950 My family and I always remain safe
3951 I'm able to retain my positive attitude around my parents
3952 It's okay to retain my individuality around my kids
3953 It's okay to hold beliefs different from my parents'
3954 I enjoy spending time with my parents
3955 My children are sweet and precious to me
3956 My children are a joy to me
3957 I have a wonderful family and it's a wonderful day
3958 I find hidden treasures within my loved ones
3959 I'm an integral part of my family
3960 I enjoy watching my children play
3961 Soon my children will move on, I show them love now
3962 I choose this day to enjoy my children's presence
3963 I always create a comfortable environment for my family
3964 I love to watch my children becoming more independent
3965 My family, friends and I all receive abundance now
3966 I deserve to see joy on my children's faces
3967 I've decided how very important my family is to me
3968 My parents love me in their own way
3969 Being adopted is part of my path
3970 I bring up my children to be caring, loving, and joyful
3971 I have confidence in my kids' strength
3972 I'm a safe place for my friends to come and share
3973 I'm always proud of my parents
3974 I'm always proud of my children
3975 I treasure the time I spend alone with my children

Patience

It's tempting to quote the old saying here: *"I want patience, and I want it right now!"*, but I won't lower myself to that. Wait... oh well, moving on...

It's important when focusing on patience to NOT focus on NEEDING MORE patience, for then you'll find yourself in circumstances in which you can test yourself on how to overcome impatience. Use affirmations as if you are already the master of your emotions; it works much quicker and easier.

3976 I choose to be patient with and kind to myself today
3977 My patience is an attribute
3978 I have much patience and understanding
3979 I possess deep patience
3980 I now have the patience I've admired in others
3981 Today I stay patient through all things
3982 I have patience to spare
3983 I find the time to be patient today
3984 I am the epitome of patience
3985 I am patient with myself and others today
3986 Patience is my middle name today and always
3987 I'm patient with allowing myself to forgive myself
3988 Patience is easy when you're living in the moment
3989 I give all patience and time thoughts over to God
3990 I am patient with my lack of patience
3991 I remain patient in all areas of my life today
3992 I'm patient with myself and my insecurities
3993 My patience is wearing thick
3994 Life is a test of my patience and I pass with flying colors
3995 Patience and I are now good friends
3996 I appreciate the patience of others today

Peace / Joy / Happiness

So, Peace, Joy and Happiness walk into a bar...
Hmmm, no, that doesn't work. Oh well, this subject is
so easy to understand, it doesn't need any formal
introduction.

3997 I am always safe and protected
3998 Peace embraces me today
3999 I'm happier than I've ever been
4000 I deserve to be peaceful
4001 I deserve to be serene
4002 It's okay to be happy
4003 It's okay to say I'm happy
4004 I give myself permission to be relaxed and happy
4005 With every breath I become more peaceful
4006 Peace surrounds me in all that I do
4007 The more love and peace I extend, the more I receive
4008 I continue to be happy
4009 I deserve a peaceful life now
4010 Living brings me great joy
4011 I spread joy with every step I take on my journey
4012 It's okay to choose to be happy
4013 It's okay to share my happy experiences with others
4014 If others share happiness with me, that's okay
4015 I deserve to be totally happy
4016 I can share my joy with others
4017 Helping others brings me great joy
4018 I am happy now, in this moment
4019 I concentrate on thoughts that make me happy
4020 I am happy and well-rested
4021 Joy is an emotion I choose to feel often
4022 I choose to live happily ever after
4023 I find joy in even the littlest things in life
4024 To retain my joy, I give it away
4025 I deserve to be around happy, joyful people

4026 I feel peaceful and joyful
4027 I am happy and content in this moment
4028 It's all right to shine with happiness
4029 Bathing gives me peace and comfort
4030 I am guilt-free about being happy
4031 I create peace and harmony for myself
4032 The fact is, I'm happy
4033 I accept peace into every facet of my existence
4034 I prove to myself that my happiness is here to stay
4035 I float along happily in my world
4036 I choose to live a peaceful life today
4037 It's okay to be happy when others are not
4038 I choose to remain calm today no matter what
4039 I breathe in peace
4040 Choosing to be happy is always okay
4041 I'm happy; hooray for me!
4042 The bottom line is, I'm peaceful
4043 I am happiness and I send forth happiness
4044 I prove to everyone that it's okay to be peaceful
4045 I depend upon only myself for my happiness
4046 It's a happy world and I intend to be part of it
4047 Happiness and I get along very well
4048 I give myself permission to be happy
4049 It's a great joy to experience life
4050 I'm happy because... I say so
4051 I'm happy with the way my mind works
4052 I choose to have a calm and peaceful demeanor
4053 I'm extremely happy with myself and with others
4054 I have the power to make myself happy
4055 I let peace penetrate every cell of my being
4056 I am relaxed and happy and so is everyone around me
4057 My life is wonderful and I share my joy with others
4058 I trust myself to remain happy today
4059 Remaining happy and positive benefits me and others
4060 My day is filled with happy surprises
4061 I live my life in peace

4062 There's always another chance to be happy
4063 Every day I discover more of what makes me joyful
4064 I see myself as having a calm, relaxed personality
4065 I resonate with power, peace and love
4066 My dominant thought is peace
4067 I give myself permission to be happy and successful
4068 Reading brings me great joy
4069 Laughter is contagious, I spread some joy today
4070 I accept all kinds of news with peace and an open mind
4071 Happiness is a culmination of a lot of little things
4072 I'm happy now, in this moment, which is all there is
4073 I'm driven to become more peaceful daily
4074 I plan to stay peaceful today
4075 Peace cascades through me like a waterfall
4076 I enjoy the basic joys of life
4077 My joyful feelings last forever
4078 I'm very happy to be here
4079 Today, I prove to myself that I can be peaceful
4080 I pay attention to the joy that surrounds me
4081 It's okay to be happy for no particular reason
4082 All my life stories have happy endings
4083 My mind is made up; I deserve to be happy and joyful
4084 Being happy and calm helps my complexion
4085 I enjoy seeing the people in my world being happy
4086 I dilute my deep thinking with lots of laughter and joy
4087 I reap what I sow and I sow peace and love
4088 I am grateful and constantly at peace
4089 I'm determined to stay peaceful today
4090 It's okay to be deliriously happy
4091 It's a joy to hear children's laughter
4092 My reaction to life is one of pure joy
4093 The decision for peace is always the right decision
4094 Forever happy and peaceful, that's my choice
4095 Peace descends all around me now and always
4096 I'm happy to be who I am, where I am and when I am
4097 I am happy in this moment and for all time

4098 In this moment, I choose to experience joy
4099 I'm now happy and well adjusted
4100 It's okay to feel peaceful about having power
4101 I'm dedicated to being happy today
4102 I'm extremely happy with the superb choices I make
4103 I'm very happy to be involved in this thing called life
4104 I breathe in peace and a new intelligence now
4105 I am, by every stretch of the imagination, happy today
4106 Today I choose to feel the rewarding feeling of peace
4107 Being happy is a decision I've made today

Politics

If you want to start a fight with somebody… start talking politics. However, it's important to remember, that no matter how vast our differences of opinion are on this subject, we can all send love to everything political. Yes, this includes that person in office who drives you crazy. Love heals; hate breeds more hate. Send love and healing to any form of politics and to all politicians today.

4108 The government and I get along very well
4109 I choose to be more politically aware this year
4110 I choose the next president with confidence
4111 All political parties now come together in peace
4112 I'm now free from being afraid of politicians
4113 It's okay to express my political views
4114 I choose to be free of resentment toward political figures
4115 I choose to be politically aware now
4116 I refuse to believe in a corrupt political system
4117 Loving people are taking a more active role in politics
4118 I'm a loving person, so I take an active role in politics
4119 Any political views I express, I express with love
4120 I send light and energy to all government officials
4121 Honest souls are being voted into government now
4122 I feel the world coming together to work for world peace
4123 Political figures are becoming kinder and smarter daily
4124 I continue to pray for all political figures on a daily basis
4125 It's okay I have different political views than my parents
4126 It's okay to have the political views that I have
4127 I can afford to have my individual political opinions
4128 I calmly listen to the political opinions of others
4129 I write my congressperson on issues I care about
4130 I send energy, peace and clear thinking to politicians

Pregnancy

Did you know that I have three kids? The twins are 22 years old and my youngest is 15 at the time of this printing, but I vividly remember when they were inside of my tummy during my pregnancy. It's a magical time that sometimes gets messed up with morning sickness and pains, but staying focused and doing a few affirmations will keep you happy to be a new Mom.

4131 I enjoy feeling new life growing inside me
4132 I'm now free from morning sickness
4133 I only gain the amount of weight I choose
4134 My pregnancy remains free of any complications
4135 My baby is growing correctly and is healthy
4136 I treat myself very well while I'm pregnant
4137 It's okay when others pamper me now
4138 It's okay when I pamper myself now
4139 My body is free of stretch marks and remains that way
4140 I've decided my body deserves to be treated well
4141 It's okay to rest more now that I'm pregnant
4142 Keeping a healthy body weight is easy for me
4143 I'm thankful I'm able to have children
4144 I enjoy being pregnant
4145 The entire birthing process is fun and exciting
4146 My unborn baby and I are forming a bond already
4147 It's easy for me to eat healthy foods for me and my baby
4148 I remember to take my prenatal vitamins
4149 My pregnancy is a joy to me
4150 Watching my body fill with a child makes me happy
4151 I get plenty of vitamins and calcium while pregnant
4152 Being a mother is a reality for me
4153 I'm thrilled to be a part of experiencing new life
4154 My baby's life is precious, so I treat myself well
4155 My life is precious, so I treat myself well

Rape / Abuse

When I was 19 years old, I was raped. It messed me up for a while. I had one abusive relationship after another. If you are stuck in this type of cycle, there is always a way out. Begin to love yourself and forgive your abuser. It's the quickest way out.

4156 I send love and energy to all who are abused
4157 I let go of any past abuse I've suffered
4158 I become more beautiful to myself every day
4159 I am now free from ever being sexually harassed
4160 The world is free from any kind of sexual harassment
4161 I'm free from feeling ashamed of being raped
4162 I transform hate to love today, for my sake
4163 My heart goes out to those who feel the need to attack
4164 I send love to my attackers, as love breeds love
4165 I can transform my feelings of anger to compassion
4166 I have many who support and love me
4167 I am able to feel clean again
4168 I release myself from feeling the attack was my fault
4169 I release myself from feeling like a victim
4170 I ask myself today what I learn from this attack situation
4171 I pray today for my attackers and for myself
4172 Today I choose to find others who understand how I feel
4173 Support groups help me find my way again now
4174 Thank God for those willing to lend love and support
4175 Even now, I see the genuine goodness of humankind
4176 I still believe there is good in everyone
4177 I accept the miracle of feelings of forgiveness
4178 I ask for, and receive, miraculous healing today
4179 I'm beginning to be able to trust men again
4180 I pray for the attacker in all of us
4181 May we all replace attacker tendencies with love
4182 I relinquish the negative energy behind my molestation
4183 Today is the day I heal from any sexual molestation

4184 I am free from feeling like a freak or alone
4185 I'm free from hatred toward my sexual attacker
4186 I reclaim my power after my sexual molestation
4187 I choose today to stand up and say NO
4188 The Universe supports me in my decision to say no
4189 The Universe supports me to be free of abuse
4190 I choose to be free of abuse now and always

Relationships / Friendships

No, you can't change the lives of others with the use of affirmations. However, you can change how you relate TO others, and draw to you the kinds of relationships you want.

4191 I am worthy of loving relationships
4192 I am drawing unto me loving relationships
4193 Loving relationships come easily to me
4194 I attract wonderful, positive people into my world
4195 I deserve lots of friends
4196 I release my friends to lead their own lives
4197 I bless and heal all relationships in my life
4198 Friendships come easily to me
4199 My friends are legion
4200 Getting out to meet people is easy for me
4201 I enjoy the company of whomever I'm with
4202 I form nurturing relationships
4203 I'm honored to have so many friends in my life
4204 I deserve to make friends with positive people
4205 I deserve to find my soul-mate
4206 I deserve to find the perfect mate for me
4207 I deserve the love of a good man
4208 I deserve the love of a good woman
4209 I choose to be accepted by my peers
4210 Everyone in my world loves and supports me
4211 I'm so in love right now, with my true Self
4212 I am romantically fulfilled
4213 It's okay to have my friendships change
4214 I communicate effectively with everyone
4215 My relationships touch my heart in a loving way
4216 All strangers I meet quickly become my friends
4217 I've earned the respect of all my friends and family
4218 I expect great relationships; so that's what I receive
4219 My date book is filled with wonderful and exciting events

4220 People find me intellectually stimulating
4221 Loving people easily find me
4222 I cherish my family while they're still living
4223 I have wonderful, supportive friends.
4224 I have very trustworthy friends
4225 I always have friends I can count on
4226 My friends can always count on me
4227 I get married at exactly the right time of my life
4228 Choosing my friends is my business
4229 Whenever I speak of others, I speak well of them
4230 I take charge and make correct dating choices
4231 I enjoy having silver and golden wedding anniversaries
4232 I'm always there when my friends need me
4233 My friends are always there when I need them
4234 My marital status is exactly as it should be at this time
4235 I visualize meeting the perfect mate for me today
4236 I keep my personal power when in all relationships
4237 I trust my mate completely
4238 I have a wonderful relationship with my sister(s)
4239 I have a wonderful relationship with my brother(s)
4240 Whatever happens, my family stays close
4241 My family and friends are a delight to me
4242 I deserve to find my significant other
4243 I deserve a loving, supportive partner
4244 I collect priceless friendships regularly
4245 I converse well with all kinds of people
4246 I have complete faith in my friends
4247 I release myself from worrying about my friends' actions
4248 My friends are always generous to me
4249 I trust that my friends always speak the truth
4250 I do favors for people, and people do favors for me
4251 I nourish my relationships with love and caring
4252 I'm content with the state of my romantic life
4253 I remain loyal to my family and friends
4254 I deserve romantic nights filled with candles and roses
4255 I deserve to find the love of my life now

4256 I'm grateful for my uniquely wonderful family
4257 I have enough time in my busy schedule for a social life
4258 I talk openly with my mate about my wants and needs
4259 My friends include me in their plans
4260 I'm comfortable doing things by myself
4261 I'm comfortable doing things in a group
4262 It's okay to do the dance of life with many partners
4263 Relationship issues become easier for me to handle
4264 I choose which people I bring into my consciousness
4265 I'm becoming more romantic every day
4266 I now find the mate I've been waiting for
4267 I now feel I deserve a loving and supportive mate
4268 I now find a mentally stable mate to love
4269 It's okay to go on a blind date if I choose
4270 When on a date, I always have a good time
4271 I deserve a mate who's faithful to me
4272 I sense the presence of friendly people all the time
4273 I'm entitled to a social life
4274 I find and meet the person I'm a romantic match for
4275 I'm happy with all of my current relationships
4276 Joy-filled relationships come easily to me now
4277 I'm free from being lonely with so many people close by
4278 I always meet the most interesting people
4279 I now choose to fall in love again
4280 My mate and I have a deep mutual understanding
4281 I treat my friends and enemies with equal love
4282 I have a man in my life who loves me and my children
4283 I have a woman who loves me and my children
4284 My marital status is changing to my liking
4285 It's easy for me to mingle with people at parties
4286 True love is available to me now and always
4287 My spouse loves me as much as I love my spouse
4288 It's possible for me to love happily ever after
4289 It's okay to love more than one person at a time
4290 I have high quality friendships
4291 Talking to strangers is becoming easier for me

4292 It's okay to have a mate who is my complete opposite
4293 It's okay to have a mate who is very much like me
4294 It's okay to be choosy concerning the people I date
4295 I'm now able to take long walks with someone special
4296 I love all my friends, even those who disagree with me
4297 It's easy for me to make new friends when I move
4298 To the opposite sex I'm very desirable
4299 I choose to be involved with good-hearted people
4300 I choose to remain neutral when my friends fight
4301 I choose my relationships on more than just looks now
4302 I find it easier now to ask people out on dates
4303 I'm honored to have the friends I have in my life
4304 It's okay to say goodbye to relationships when it's time
4305 I choose to improve the relationship I have with myself
4306 I feel unchanging, unconditional love toward my spouse
4307 I've decided to help make my marriage work
4308 I'm very good at being happily married
4309 The people that I'm with make all experiences delightful
4310 I'm okay with diligently working on a relationship
4311 I have now found someone who loves me for who I am
4312 I'm ready to find my companion today
4313 I now enjoy peaceful relationships
4314 I form relationships quickly, as I'm more myself now
4315 Letting old relationships fall away is a natural part of life
4316 I release myself from the guilt of ending a relationship
4317 Making the choice to end a relationship is all right
4318 I have healthy relationships in all areas of my life now
4319 I have a positive-minded mate
4320 I have a mate who shares my interests and passions
4321 My friends are exactly who I need in my life
4322 When friendships end, I send them peace
4323 I decide how to view the ending of a relationship
4324 I choose to be romantic today
4325 My friends are my sunshine on rainy days
4326 My love life continues to get better and better
4327 I notice, applaud and honor the friends in my life

4328 Through relationships I learn to know myself better
4329 Time spent in the company of my friends is precious
4330 I respect my partner's views
4331 My friends are free to be themselves around me
4332 I concentrate on my friends' good qualities
4333 It's okay to be choosy when picking a mate

Retirement

My parents recently retired and are REALLY enjoying their time together. It can be a beautiful time of life, where you re-discover what you truly love to do. Remember to enjoy it!

4334 I'm now free to enjoy my retirement
4335 I deserve to spend these years taking it easy
4336 I happily retire earlier than I had planned
4337 I can easily afford being retired
4338 My lifestyle is very luxurious, even through retirement
4339 It's easier for me to relax and enjoy retirement
4340 My passion for life continues through my retirement
4341 Spending time with family and friends is invigorating
4342 I'm glad to be able to spend more time with my hobbies
4343 I discover new areas of interest, now that I'm retired
4344 Having time to do whatever I want is very freeing
4345 Time away from work brings me joy and freedom
4346 I have new adventures ahead of me
4347 Being retired is only part of who I am
4348 I now make friendships with other retired persons
4349 I enjoy having time to pursue whatever I please
4350 I remain financially stable throughout my retirement
4351 I can now sleep late and I deserve it
4352 My health remains excellent all through retirement
4353 I have excellent health insurance that I can easily afford
4354 My need for medication is diminishing
4355 I experience exciting new challenges in my retirement
4356 In my retirement I'm taking time to help others

Safety

It's best to assume you are safe, not focus and worry about your safety. However, if you find yourself feeling unsafe, affirmations can help to bring you out of it.

4357 I am always safe and protected
4358 I am safe at all times
4359 I easily avoid dangerous circumstances
4360 I deserve to be safe at all times
4361 I see myself safely traveling to and from work every day
4362 God keeps me well protected, and I feel that today
4363 Held safely within me are the answers to my questions
4364 I am safe within myself
4365 I am safe within my thoughts
4366 I remain safe through my entire spiritual journey
4367 Earth is now a safe place to live
4368 It's safe to openly express my ideas
4369 I'm free from feeling I need to be physically protected
4370 I am safe from all people who would try to hurt me
4371 I deserve a safe environment
4372 My safety is assured
4373 My family and I remain safe always
4374 Worry thoughts about my safety are gone
4375 I continue to live safely, among well-adjusted people

Senior Citizens / Middle Age

I occasionally teach computers at our local technical college. Many of my students are senior citizens, and I love them dearly. I enjoy their life experiences, and the fact that they are still reaching out for learning all through their lives. I'm 47 at the time of this printing, so I guess that qualifies me for middle-age. It's just a label society tries to place on us. We can accept it or not. Live each day to the fullest at any and all ages.

4376 I bless all the years that I've lived
4377 I deserve to live my life pain-free
4378 I deserve to feel young
4379 I deserve to act young, even when others don't
4380 It's okay to be healthy when others around me are ill
4381 I enjoy being elderly at this time in my life
4382 I am having the best years of my life
4383 It's okay to live my senior years medication-free
4384 It's okay to be proud of living so long
4385 I have contributed much to my world
4386 Every day I live, I contribute to the world
4387 I choose to live the remainder of this life in total comfort
4388 I live the remainder of this life in total happiness
4389 I feel a renewed energy every day
4390 All my organs are as strong and healthy as ever
4391 My mental capacities grow stronger every day
4392 I draw people unto me who need me and my skills
4393 There is plenty of room on the planet for me to exist
4394 I am worthy of being a part of this planet
4395 There is plenty of time for all I still choose to do
4396 I'm proud to be a senior citizen
4397 I deserve to live for a very long time
4398 I contribute to the world at any age
4399 I feel younger now than I did in my 20s (insert number)
4400 As the years go on, I find continued joy and purpose

4401 My spine stays strong and supple
4402 I retain my faculties even unto old age
4403 My hair remains a vibrant color, free from gray
4404 I retain excellent driving skills even unto older ages
4405 I love my gray hair; it makes me look distinguished
4406 I think I'm young, so I am
4407 My young friends help keep me younger
4408 As I'm aging I'm gaining wisdom
4409 I'm keeping fit to better enjoy my golden years
4410 When I hear my grandchildren sing, my heart smiles
4411 Listening to my children laugh makes my heart sing
4412 I keep my mind and body active to remain young
4413 Life is more precious to me as the years go by
4414 Age is only a number to me
4415 I choose to feel, act, and look young
4416 I've lived many years and am enjoying my memories
4417 When I stay fit physically and mentally, I stay young
4418 My children and grandchildren bring sunshine to my life
4419 It's okay to continue to grow wiser as I mature
4420 Others may think I'm old, yet I'm out-walking them
4421 Learning new things keeps me young
4422 New mental challenges keep my mind young
4423 I am thankful for the ability to learn new things
4424 It's a pleasure to be a role model to my grandchildren
4425 I am keeping my mind fertile by exercising it
4426 My gray hair is beautiful and I love it

Serious Illness

This is a serious subject, of course, as it's no fun (and down-right scary) to get diagnosed with having a serious illness. However, one person's opinion of your body does NOT make it true. You are always able to turn that around and help heal yourself. For those of you reading this section, please also read the section on Healing.

4427 I am free of AIDS
4428 I'm free from feeling anybody deserves to get an illness
4429 My body is free from what people call AIDS or HIV
4430 My body performs in a healthy manner 100% of the time
4431 My body is now free from what is called heart disease
4432 I am free from ever having the condition of a stroke
4433 I choose to remain free from all life-threatening illnesses
4434 I believe my illness and all illnesses will be healed
4435 I allow myself to be healed today
4436 I breathe love into my illness and watch it disappear
4437 There's always time to start and complete my destiny
4438 It's okay to believe that this illness is part of my destiny
4439 I believe curing this illness is part of my destiny
4440 I release the disease now
4441 I choose to release this disease to the Universe
4442 I still have time to be cured, and I am
4443 I'm free from believing that doctors know more than I
4444 I believe in positive outcomes, even if I'm the only one
4445 I send love to those who've given me a death sentence
4446 I send love to doctors who believe I'm being optimistic
4447 I send love and energy to the doctors who laugh at me
4448 I use holistic healing practices now, with great results
4449 The power of prayer is more powerful than doctors
4450 My body is free from any effects of Leukemia
4451 My lungs remain clear of anything called Emphysema
4452 My blood has all the cells it needs to fight off disease

4453 I choose to send my healing body love today
4454 Healing is my choice, I accept it now
4455 I accept the healing light from the Universe today
4456 I ask for, and accept, healing from my Divine Source
4457 Today I am healed, in the blink of an eye
4458 Today I find myself in perfect health, completely healed
4459 I laugh with joy as I watch my body being healed
4460 Since we all need healing, I send out healing love today
4461 I am healed of the desire to remain ill
4462 Being healed is my right, and I accept it now
4463 All miracles are equal; I accept the miracle of health
4464 Today I visualize the healing taking place in my body
4465 I see my cancer cells breaking up and disappearing
4466 I always believe everything is curable
4467 I am free of Cancer
4468 I am healthier every day
4469 With every breath I become stronger and healthier
4470 I am victorious over all diseases
4471 I choose to be healthy
4472 My body is free from what people call Cancer
4473 I choose to be disease-free
4474 I deserve to be healthy
4475 I deserve to feel wonderful every day
4476 I am worthy of being healthy and happy
4477 There is room for me on this planet
4478 I live to a very old age, full of good health and joy
4479 I've released any fear surrounding the AIDS virus

Sexual Challenges

Some people are comfortable with their sexuality, and others are not. I urge you to read through this section if you are having issues in this area.

4480 I am easily able to handle my sexuality
4481 It's okay to have sexual feelings
4482 I forgive myself for being sexually active
4483 I forgive those want me to think sex is wrong
4484 I am able to choose my sexual partners responsibly
4485 My sexuality is a part of me
4486 My urges are natural
4487 Every day I love myself more
4488 It's okay to be homosexual
4489 It's okay to be heterosexual
4490 Being homosexual is part of what makes me unique
4491 Being heterosexual is part of what makes me unique
4492 It's okay my parents don't agree with my sexual choices
4493 I'm a great person who happens to be sexually active
4494 I am free from negative comments about my sexuality
4495 My love life brings me much happiness
4496 I draw positive, caring relationships into my life
4497 Being bi-sexual is only a part of the whole of who I am
4498 I meet people who are open to my ideas of sexuality
4499 I love myself no matter what
4500 It's all right to ignore the comments of others
4501 I forgive everyone who tries to torment me
4502 When negative feelings arise, I breathe into them
4503 I deserve to live my life to the fullest
4504 I am free of stereotypical comments and attitudes
4505 I am worthy of retaining my perfect health
4506 I draw honest, open people into my world
4507 I am completely confident in my skills as a lover
4508 I always remember to practice safe sex
4509 I am sexually responsible

4510 I always use my chosen birth control method
4511 I'm easily sexually satisfied
4512 I keep my sexual desires under control
4513 I deserve to have great sex
4514 Touching others helps me to connect with them today
4515 My decision to remain a virgin at this time is right for me
4516 It's okay to be a virgin at any age
4517 I'm a very good kisser
4518 I protect myself from sexually transmitted diseases
4519 I've decided to plan when to become a parent
4520 I choose to relinquish any sexual addictions I may have
4521 Monogamy is a great turn-on
4522 It's okay to choose abstinence as a birth control method
4523 I choose to remain careful regarding birth control
4524 I have chosen to relinquish the selling of my body
4525 It's okay that I've accepted money for sex in this lifetime
4526 I release all feelings of guilt surrounding sex
4527 The desire to be a prostitute is now gone from my mind
4528 I'm now free from the desire to sell my body for money

Single Parents

Boy, could I write a book on this subject. Actually, I did write a chapter in a James Twyman book on the subject of raising children. The trials and exhaustion (and joys) that come from being a single parent, only another single parent truly understands. For any single parents reading this, my heart and love goes out to you. It's a tough job, but very, very rewarding.

4529 It's okay to be a single parent
4530 God gives strength to single parents
4531 Single parents are brave; I'm brave and courageous
4532 I find time to have a social life
4533 I have kind, caring, affordable sitters whenever I choose
4534 I have those who are willing to help when necessary
4535 Being a single parent is part of who I am
4536 Any stigmas about being a single parent are gone
4537 The choice I made to be a single parent is a good one
4538 I enjoy being single and having children
4539 My children and I cut each other some slack today
4540 Being a single parent is part of what makes me unique
4541 My children and I form a strong bond
4542 I meet interesting, positive-minded single parents
4543 I form new friendships quickly and easily
4544 I send love and blessings to single parents

Sleep Challenges

It seems that sleep challenges are on the rise. (no pun intended). Stress can cause many of us to have trouble sleeping, as our brains run non-stop trying to figure out all the intricacies of our lives. Sleep is a time to shut all of that out and relax into recuperative sleep. If you're having trouble sleeping soundly, it's time to claim it back again.

4545 Positive thoughts penetrate my thinking while I sleep
4546 My sleep is always restful
4547 Getting to sleep quickly is easy for me
4548 When I get little sleep, I still perform in top form
4549 Tonight I lay all worries aside before going to sleep
4550 Nightmares are a part of my past and I release them
4551 Should a bad dream begin, I easily release it
4552 I program my mind to accept positive dreams
4553 I have the power to release any negative dreams
4554 I'm determined to dream only happy, positive dreams
4555 I learn valuable insights from my dreams
4556 I always remember my dreams
4557 My dreams reveal important past and future events
4558 Dreaming is always pleasant for me
4559 I'm able to fall asleep quickly and peacefully
4560 I sleep soundly and peacefully
4561 I'm able to stop all worrying before going to sleep
4562 Any and all sleep disorders I now release from me
4563 I always sleep the exact number of hours I need
4564 I always have plenty of time to get a good night's sleep
4565 My bed is always comfortable
4566 I release myself of the affliction of night sweats
4567 I'm able to wake up with my bed still dry
4568 I now sleep all the way through the night peacefully
4569 I'm now free of any bladder-control problems
4570 I remember to say my affirmations before bedtime

4571 My nighttime routine helps enable me to drift off to sleep
4572 I release last night's bad dreams and any fears to God
4573 Even on little sleep, my motor skills remain excellent
4574 I choose now to dream only happy, joyful dreams
4575 In the light of day all nightmares disappear
4576 I choose to have an easy time falling asleep tonight
4577 Sleep disorders are a thing of the past for me
4578 I visualize positive images before retiring tonight
4579 It's okay to completely relax every night
4580 It's okay to get a good night sleep every night
4581 I deserve to feel well-rested

Spiritual Matters

You will find many variations of spiritual talk in this section. Sometimes I use the word "God", other times "Holy Spirit", other times "Great Spirit" and still other times "Universe". Choose whatever feels correct to you within your belief system.

4582 Tonight I choose to cuddle up with a good prayer
4583 My search for God is ultimately successful
4584 I choose to hear what God wants me to hear today
4585 I thank you Holy Spirit for the divine in all of us
4586 I empty my hands to allow for God's next move
4587 I accept the life roles God has given me
4588 I steadfastly adhere to my spiritual beliefs
4589 I'm now open-minded about my spiritual beliefs
4590 I allow God to light my path, with really bright bulbs
4591 Living by God's grace is living a marvelous existence
4592 My power is in my willingness to release control to God
4593 The healing light of God surrounds me
4594 My heart is overflowing with thankfulness to God
4595 God is at work in my life today
4596 I thank God for the sunshine today
4597 I thank God for the rain today
4598 I give all worry thoughts over to God
4599 I am calmly enjoying God's presence
4600 I accept the gifts God extends unto me
4601 I deserve to fulfill God's plan for me
4602 Whenever I need help, God provides assistance
4603 God works through me and my happiness
4604 God wants me to be happy at all times
4605 I love God and God loves me
4606 God wants me to succeed and prosper
4607 God supports me in all I say and do
4608 I am an heir to spiritual royalty
4609 I accept my inheritance from my father, the King

4610 I accept my inheritance from my mother, the Goddess
4611 God carries me over every hurdle
4612 I easily communicate with angelic beings
4613 I'm worthy of communicating with my spirit guides
4614 I deserve to know God's plan for me
4615 I have great fun performing miracles with God
4616 I allow my Creator to lead me
4617 I stand aside and let Divine Intervention lead me
4618 God has my best interests at heart
4619 Any friend of God's is a friend of mine
4620 Holy Spirit is always with me
4621 My purpose is revealed to me moment by moment
4622 I accept my inheritance from my Creator
4623 I am willing to accept my gifts from my Creator
4624 Holy Spirit, I release this day unto you
4625 Holy Spirit, make my mind pure and loving
4626 I let my actions reflect the love that is my essence
4627 Holy Spirit, I open my mind and my heart to you
4628 I give all my worries over to God
4629 I give all my fears to Holy Spirit to handle from now on
4630 Delegating my fears to Holy Spirit frees me
4631 I thank God that I'm able to breathe deeply
4632 My limitlessness is a gift from God
4633 The healing light of God surrounds me
4634 I release all my hopes and fears to Divine Guidance
4635 I exist because I am important to God
4636 God reveals mysteries to me every day
4637 Answers to my questions are given me from my Creator
4638 I give my depression over to a higher power
4639 God is my friend
4640 Holy Spirit always has time for me
4641 The phrase Spiritual Life is redundant
4642 My spiritual life provides strength and comfort
4643 My spiritual life is important to me and I'm unashamed
4644 My faith carries me through all things
4645 I am open to suggestions from God

4646 I come across to others the way God intended
4647 I deserve to do God's work
4648 I'm an integral part of God's plan
4649 It feels great to be loved by God
4650 God wants me to prosper, and I do
4651 I am God's wondrous creation
4652 I rejoice in what God has given me
4653 I know what God wants for me
4654 I know what God wants me to do and I'm doing it
4655 I am illuminated in God's light
4656 What God reveals to me today is magnificent
4657 I'm entitled to my inheritance
4658 I choose to know the will of God for me
4659 I start a new phase in my spiritual development today
4660 My hunches and gut feelings are God speaking to me
4661 My intuition is a gift from God
4662 God helps me to set the perfect schedule for my days
4663 I thank God for my increasing self-confidence
4664 Prayer is always the answer
4665 Praying lightens my soul
4666 Arguing is an activity I've given over to God
4667 Time spent in prayer is time well spent
4668 Holy Spirit, I accept your influence in my life
4669 Receiving guidance from my Creator is natural
4670 I love the life God has given me
4671 Total cooperation is what I give God today
4672 I pray that I hold my temper at bay today
4673 Today I choose to speak with reverence to my Creator
4674 Today I choose to speak with joy to my Creator
4675 My chosen religion brings me great comfort
4676 God gets us through all dark days
4677 We all have eternal life
4678 Since ultimately my boss is God, I've got a great boss
4679 Holy Spirit, I accept all the good you offer me now
4680 God, please show me what to learn in this situation
4681 I stay positive around those who are not

4682 Since I am part of God and God is love, I am love
4683 No matter what, I remain an innocent child of God
4684 I allow my beliefs, and I allow the beliefs of others
4685 I'm free from having to believe as someone else does
4686 I am free to believe what I choose
4687 I remain calm and centered when expressing my beliefs
4688 My beliefs are as true for me as yours are for you
4689 My beliefs are as right as any other notion
4690 My beliefs are perfect for me
4691 I believe that my beliefs are good
4692 No matter what, I know I have my faith
4693 My faith gets me through everything
4694 God designed me perfectly to fulfill my mission on Earth
4695 I think God is cool, and God thinks I'm cool too
4696 I accept help from my angels
4697 I am free from being afraid of angelic beings
4698 I feel the love that comes from the angels around me
4699 I thank God for the energy I've been given today
4700 I thank God for all inspirational thoughts
4701 Spirituality has a positive influence over my life
4702 In every situation, my faith stays strong
4703 In all things my faith holds firm
4704 I lct God make adjustments in my life
4705 I release all negative situations to you, Holy Spirit
4706 When I'm tempted to react with anger, I ask God's help
4707 I surrender to God's guidance and compassion
4708 I've decided to do things God's way
4709 I remember to read spiritual lessons each day
4710 God leads me to the reading materials that help me
4711 I give any murderous thoughts over to God
4712 Every day God gives me proof of my worth
4713 Time spent communicating with God is time well spent
4714 I allow the heavy feeling in my stomach to disappear
4715 I thank God for my increased energy flow
4716 I thank God for all things now and in the future
4717 I prepare myself for God's guidance

4718 I'm willing to do whatever God wills
4719 God and I have great plans for my future
4720 I now sense the presence of angels around me
4721 Following God's will is a habit for me now
4722 Consulting with God on daily issues comes easily
4723 I pray that I retain the lessons I learn today
4724 God gives many visual aides to help me through life
4725 I thank God for my peace of mind today
4726 I draw strength from God today
4727 I give all weakness thoughts over to God now
4728 I am powerful in God's love
4729 I believe my prayers are answered now and always
4730 I pray for clarity of mind to understand God's messages
4731 I thank God for every idea that becomes manifest
4732 I ask God for help with my anger and disappointment
4733 God wills the very best for me
4734 Tough choices become easier with God's guidance
4735 God's energy heals all things
4736 It's normal and natural to believe in miracles
4737 I've decided to forgive and forget any past indiscretions
4738 All my prayers are answered today
4739 Today I take a hint; God really wants me to be happy
4740 I depend upon my angels for guidance and that's okay
4741 I'm thankful for all God has given me to do
4742 I thank God for the dedication I feel toward my work
4743 I now let God sort out all the details of my life
4744 Holy Spirit reveals to me my purpose now
4745 I'm patient with the speed of my spiritual growth
4746 I have complete religious freedom
4747 I now accept God's influence in my life
4748 I offer my stillness to God today
4749 I choose to be led to the mind of God
4750 God holds my hand when I ask
4751 God has given me everything and freedom to choose it
4752 I place my day in the hands of God
4753 Today I realize the true love of God

4754 I now give to my Creator any mistakes I've made
4755 My faith increases several degrees each day
4756 God, I now choose to breathe in your wisdom
4757 I extend the love of God today
4758 I see God in everything
4759 There is sacredness inside of me
4760 Today I discover my God-given functions
4761 I, as a child of God, possess a certain dignity and grace
4762 I now relax and let God take the wheel
4763 When my mind is quiet I can better hear God's voice
4764 God is gently pushing me forward toward my destiny
4765 I am your willing vessel, God, fill me up and use me
4766 I have enough energy to do all that I choose in this life
4767 I am grateful for God's help in completing my mission
4768 I am confident and God loves it
4769 I deserve the blessings I receive
4770 I thank you God for the spiritual high you've given me
4771 I decide to receive instructions from God every day
4772 God is a great travel agent
4773 I choose to leave all travel planning up to God
4774 I choose today to read God's instructions loud and clear
4775 I let the final decision rest with God
4776 I choose to be chosen by God for great things
4777 I love the work God has given me to do
4778 Heaven feels closer every day
4779 I now let God clear up my misperceptions
4780 I'm thrilled to be filled with the Holy Spirit
4781 I choose to consult with God often today
4782 Every time I talk to God I know I'm being heard
4783 It's possible to be spiritual and still make good money
4784 God's vitality is alive within me and my job on Earth
4785 I accept God's promises today
4786 I give only God authority over my thoughts and ideas
4787 My sisters and brothers are extensions of God
4788 Praying has become a healthy habit for me now
4789 I am part of God's light, and I contribute to the shine

4790 I am here to do the job in which God intended
4791 Every time I thank my Creator, I feel even more blessed
4792 Turning my life over to God is a freeing experience
4793 I accept the protection God freely gives
4794 I choose God's love to light my way today
4795 Today I accept what I feel a child of God deserves
4796 My faults I give over to God
4797 I'm becoming more of what God intended me to be
4798 God is a part of everything I do
4799 I thank God for the joy I'm feeling in this moment
4800 Gratitude to our Creator is always appropriate
4801 I'm relieved that God has a big eraser for my mistakes
4802 I hand over all guilt and remorse to God
4803 I grasp the hand of God today to seal our partnership
4804 I choose to rejoice with God and the Universe today
4805 I give to God any notion that I've failed today
4806 There's a fire in my soul that I blaze brightly to the world
4807 I let God lovingly stroke away my headache today
4808 I release all levels of confusion to my Creator now
4809 I'm now enjoying life as God intended
4810 God washes the old negative thoughts from my mind
4811 I thank God for the changes in my life
4812 I thank God for the lack of changes in my soul
4813 I give my shakiness over to God
4814 I give over to God my feelings that I can't handle life
4815 I have all the strength I need for any task
4816 My life is important to God
4817 My faith grows in struggles when my faith remains firm
4818 I'm lingering in God's presence, watching the sun rise
4819 God gave me talents and I'm using them daily
4820 Praying stimulates doing
4821 God is leading me through valleys to mountaintops
4822 The more I pray the closer my relationship with God
4823 My day begins and ends with God
4824 My existence is a gift from God
4825 The fact that I exist is a miracle

4826 Today I'm receiving sustenance from God
4827 My trials energize my faith
4828 God's strength sustains me when I begin to feel weak
4829 God placed me here for a special purpose
4830 My heart is overflowing with thankfulness to God
4831 God is at work in my life today
4832 I finish all projects God assigns for me today
4833 Holy Spirit, please allow me to remain calm now
4834 I choose to have fun with my spiritual training today
4835 Today I experience God's humor like a warm hug
4836 Today I choose to take many leaps of faith
4837 I give myself permission to co-create with God
4838 When in doubt, I immediately turn to God
4839 I breathe deeply the clear vision from God
4840 I empty my mind so God may fill it with information
4841 Anything is possible with God
4842 Praying with faith... it's a safe bet
4843 My ultimate assignment from God is to be myself
4844 Today I surrender my plans to God
4845 I gladly and willingly accept your advice now, God
4846 I give the hand of God a high-five today
4847 I thank you God for this feeling of contentment
4848 I choose now to accept God's promises
4849 Today I bring my feelings of anger to God
4850 When I put things into perspective, I choose to pray
4851 Today I choose to pray for all the people I don't like
4852 I choose to notice God's special delight with me
4853 I'm astounded of the talents God has given me
4854 God's tasks come with instructions; I listen today
4855 Today I allow God's love to melt my frozen feelings
4856 I give sickness of my soul over to God to heal today
4857 I trust God today to send my love where it's needed
4858 One of my greatest abilities is to follow God's advice
4859 I accept your golden healing light now, God
4860 Healing penetrates my being
4861 The will of God takes over my consciousness today

4862 I choose to see what God has given me
4863 I choose to see more of God's beauty without fear
4864 I have faith that prayers are heard and answered
4865 My abilities are strengthened because of my faith
4866 My quiet time with God is sustaining me
4867 I am accepting God's changes in my life
4868 God's guidance in my life is crucial to me

Stress

"Stress" seems to be everyone's middle name these days. In fact, if you're not looking and feeling stressed, it gives the impression to some that you're not working hard enough. Stress is NOT helpful and you will actually be LESS productive when you remain in a state of stress. Take a few moments and disconnect from the stress, and find yourself flowing through your projects with ease.

4869 Exercise provides healthy release of stress for me
4870 The pressures in my life diminish daily
4871 I breathe deeply to clear away stress
4872 When in a stressful situation, I choose to be peaceful
4873 I choose a stress-free life
4874 I release my tension with each breath
4875 I remember to relax in stressful situations
4876 I remember to do deep breathing in stressful times
4877 I'm free from feeling the need to have stress in my life
4878 Stress and I are now parting company
4879 Stress is only a perception
4880 I'm finally free from all effects of stress
4881 The desire to feel stress is now gone from my being
4882 I deserve to remain free of stress forever
4883 I release all stress thoughts to my Creator today
4884 I relinquish the habit of caving in to stress today
4885 Stress feels uncomfortable, my body chooses peace
4886 I'm finally able to say goodbye to stress forever
4887 Pressures in my life diminish daily
4888 I release my body from the need to react to stress
4889 I can easily handle pressure
4890 I remember to stretch often to release stress
4891 Doing affirmations is now a positive habit
4892 I release any stress I hold in my neck and shoulders
4893 I now release my body from any symptoms of stress

4894 I'm committed to stress-free living
4895 Taking deep breaths comes naturally to me now
4896 I mentally relax the tension out of my shoulders
4897 I feel hands of light massaging stress out of my neck

Success

What does success mean to you? Don't just look to the material and financial; cultivate success in all areas of your life.

4898 I deserve to enjoy success in all I do
4899 It's okay to succeed at my age
4900 Success comes naturally to me
4901 I am wildly successful in all of my pursuits
4902 I embrace success
4903 Where success is concerned, I am free of fear
4904 I am as deserving of success as anyone else
4905 I am always successful in all I say and do
4906 I am guilt-free about being successful
4907 Success is written on every page of my life story
4908 I am successful in extending love today
4909 I'm a success in all I say and do
4910 Success and I are on the same wavelength
4911 I deserve to remain successful
4912 I'm successful and caring
4913 I'm planning for success
4914 It's okay to succeed beyond my wildest expectations
4915 It's okay to succeed up many different avenues
4916 It's okay to be successful quickly
4917 I wish everyone success and prosperity
4918 I set myself up to succeed
4919 I'm prosperous more each day
4920 I'm prosperity-minded now
4921 Money loves me
4922 It's okay to love money; and I do
4923 Dollars flow easily to me now
4924 I frequently accept large amounts of money
4925 Money is increasing in my bank accounts
4926 Every day my dollars increase
4927 I watch with glee as money comes to me easily

4928 I effortlessly acquire more wealth
4929 My life has ever-increasing value
4930 I allow myself to accept thousands of dollars
4931 Each week I allow more financial abundance
4932 I allow abundance to flow to and through me
4933 I'm fond of money and it's fond of me
4934 This is it, my time to be rich
4935 I'm in charge of my own wealth
4936 Money flows to me in abundant amounts
4937 The time for poverty is over
4938 My future holds only abundance
4939 I'm the perfect person to receive great wealth
4940 I make a very good living
4941 I drop any walls and accept my wealth
4942 My consciousness attracts wealthy thoughts
4943 I accept my power and the wealth that it brings me
4944 I'm more affluent each day
4945 I allow my affluence
4946 I am abundant now and always
4947 I'm free from thoughts of scarcity
4948 I'm free from thoughts of limiting thoughts
4949 Floods of money come to me easily
4950 I easily and quickly manifest riches for my family
4951 Each day brings me closer to my goals being manifest
4952 I'm able to buy anything I want
4953 I find and accept prosperity at every turn
4954 I attract people who help me to my riches
4955 I help others to their riches
4956 It's holy and good to be rich
4957 I fulfill all my financial dreams now
4958 Money easily flows into my experience
4959 I laugh with glee as I release the old me
4960 Money shows me its secrets of love energy now
4961 Money is love energy in motion
4962 I now fulfill my money desires
4963 Money comes to me from unexpected sources today

4964 Everything I want to purchase, I can now
4965 My money grows in leaps and bounds
4966 I allow the Universe to treat me well today
4967 I'm special and unique and I treat myself very well
4968 With every breath, I accept and allow more abundance
4969 I feel marvelous as a rich person
4970 I'm richer and richer every day
4971 I allow myself to spontaneously become wealthy
4972 I accept financial miracles
4973 I can easily afford anything that pops into my head
4974 I realize my dream of being a millionaire now
4975 I have created a debt-free existence
4976 All my bills are paid quickly and easily
4977 I'm now free from any debt or outstanding bills
4978 I allow and listen to my Inner Financial Guide
4979 I clearly see and feel myself rich now
4980 It's a glorious feeling to be debt-free now and always
4981 I invite my Internal Financial Friend to take over now
4982 I am led by financial geniuses
4983 I still have time to become very wealthy in this lifetime
4984 My immense wealth is a "given"
4985 I accept the gift of wealth and extend wealth
4986 I send increase and prosperity to all I meet
4987 I'm so happy for all millionaires
4988 I'm a happy, healthy millionaire
4989 Life keeps getting better and better
4990 I enjoy all the doors the Universe helps me to open
4991 With every breath I relax into divine guidance
4992 I see the most joyous path, shining brightly at all times
4993 Doing what I love is a gift to the world and to me
4994 I allow things to keep getting better and more abundant
4995 I know what I want to create, and I begin to create it
4996 I'm grateful for the lessons I've gone through lately
4997 I'm so grateful for all that I have and all that I am
4998 Every moment contains great joys and I find them
4999 With every breath I allow more good from the Universe

5000 I'm making important, joyful choices
5001 I allow my feelings to show me where to focus today
5002 I allow all financial abundance I can imagine, and more
5003 I pay all bills and have plenty left over
5004 It's such a relief to finally be free of fear
5005 It feels so good to allow the best in life
5006 Each moment holds the promise of good things
5007 It's always up to me to accept the best
5008 I am rich, right now, in this moment
5009 It's okay for me to be rich, happy and healthy
5010 I now have more money than ever before
5011 Today I heal my past relationship with money
5012 I have a happy and abundant relationship with money
5013 I'm able to focus on my projects and do them well today
5014 I love myself, whether I'm poor or rich
5015 I love being rich, and the world loves me rich
5016 Now that I'm rich, I'm still able to be kind and loving
5017 I enjoy my abundant money and know it will continue
5018 It's okay to expect bigger and better things in my life
5019 I expect and accept more joy and prosperity now
5020 God wants me to be joyful and prosperous, and I accept
5021 I see my checking account bursting with extra money
5022 It's okay to allow more and more prosperity every day
5023 I love the new, abundant life I'm creating for myself
5024 Everywhere I look there is financial abundance
5025 When I'm rich, I help others, so it's good I'm rich
5026 I allow the Universe to provide lavishly for me always
5027 Money comes to me easily and consistently
5028 I have more money each day than the day before
5029 Money and I are now good friends
5030 My bills are all easily paid, with lots of money left over
5031 It's fun to have plenty of money to buy my kids clothes
5032 Today my good fortune increases
5033 Money comes quickly to me
5034 The dam has burst and money joyfully flows to me
5035 My energy and the energy of money mingle well

5036 Everything I touch turns to money
5037 I'm a successful risk-taker
5038 I can handle all aspects of success
5039 I succeed at everything I attempt today
5040 It's logical to expect success
5041 I plan to be successful today
5042 I'm instrumental to my own success
5043 Determination to succeed is one of my traits
5044 I have enough guts to succeed
5045 I have the intention to succeed
5046 I am only in competition with myself
5047 My success is possible, and probable, and I allow it
5048 I've enjoyed many things in life; I now enjoy success
5049 I'm so happy for my friends' successes
5050 I definitely deserve success
5051 I'm worthy of the experience of success
5052 I have the determination necessary to succeed
5053 I'm happy when I hear of someone's success
5054 When others worry about me, I send them love
5055 I am now certain of my ultimate success
5056 Success has a comfortable, familiar feel to it
5057 I am successful in a field in which few people are
5058 The way is laid for my success and I accept it now
5059 I remain gentle and caring as I become successful
5060 My ultimate success is happiness
5061 I'm a success because I dared to try
5062 I'm successful because I'm assertive
5063 My confidence helps me succeed
5064 Today I choose to pave my way for future successes
5065 Success is an ongoing feeling that I choose to create
5066 I take my place among those who have dared to try
5067 Today I hold the clear vision of success
5068 I choose to believe that success is here for my asking
5069 I choose to see myself as a success today
5070 My life is a continuous string of successes
5071 I am successful doing work I love

Truth / Honesty

There are those among us who have a bit of trouble in this area. If it is you, or someone you know, you might enjoy spending a bit of time here.

5072 I am a trustworthy person
5073 I attract honest and kind personalities unto me
5074 Everyone I deal with is honest and caring
5075 I tell the truth at all times
5076 Telling lies is part of my past and I release it now
5077 I remember to always tell the truth
5078 It's easier to tell the truth the first time around
5079 Speaking my truth is easy for me
5080 Expressing my truth comes easier to me each day
5081 I find honest, qualified mechanics when necessary
5082 I find honest people in all walks of life
5083 Honest, loving people are drawn to me and me to them
5084 Good things happen when I speak my truth
5085 I'm honest with people about my feelings
5086 I'm very honest and I remain that way forever
5087 I am lovingly honest and genuine
5088 I choose to tell the truth now
5089 Every day I'm becoming more honest
5090 I'm proud to be thought of as an honest person
5091 I have a habit of being completely honest

Universe

This section is devoted to focusing on the entirety of the Universe, of which you are an integral part. Breathe in and feel the expansiveness of the Universe, and feel your Oneness within it.

5092 My existence is important to the Universe
5093 I am the center of my Universe
5094 The Universe loves me and I love the Universe
5095 The Universe supports me in all of my endeavors
5096 I am loved by the Universe
5097 It's cool to be loved by the Universe
5098 Every day I do a cosmic dance with the Universe
5099 I effectively communicate with the Universe today
5100 I trust the Universe to always guide me
5101 I'm as good and deserving as anyone in the Universe
5102 I communicate with the Universe very clearly
5103 My thoughts and actions help the Universe
5104 I give the Universe an embrace within this moment
5105 I live in a Universe that supports all that I do
5106 I accept energy from the Universe now, in this moment
5107 My existence is needed by the Universe
5108 I join humanity in blowing a kiss to the Universe
5109 To experience the Universe, I need to give it a chance
5110 The Universe opens its arms to protect and love me
5111 My positive energy is good for the Universe
5112 I release any limiting beliefs to the Universe now
5113 I let the Universe take care of me
5114 I get in touch with the Universe within me
5115 I allow the Universe to guide my actions
5116 I release my anger to the Universe to be transformed
5117 I join the Universe in praying for all children in gangs
5118 My soul dances with the Universe today
5119 I always receive excellent guidance from the Universe
5120 When I increase my self-worth the Universe benefits

5121 I'm the most important person in my Universe
5122 I unfold the beauty of who I am onto the Universe
5123 I'm beginning to understand life's mysteries now
5124 I am at one with the Universe
5125 I choose to be open to guidance from the Universe
5126 I release all emotions to the Universe
5127 I breathe in positive energy from the Universe
5128 I'm comfortable within the Universe
5129 I relax and let the Universe take over
5130 I applaud the Universe
5131 I have faith in the Universe
5132 I have power over my individual Universe
5133 I accept love from the Universe
5134 I'm an asset to the Universe and I remember that today
5135 My love puts energizing power into the Universe
5136 Blessings pour from the Creator to the entire Universe
5137 I'm generous, and the Universe is generous to me
5138 I let the Universe take over and gently guide me
5139 I choose to send the Universe love and acceptance
5140 The Universe trusts me, and I trust the Universe
5141 I flamboyantly declare my love to the Universe today
5142 I learn more about the meaning of the Universe today
5143 Today I'm clear in my requests to the Universe
5144 I have the unlimited power of the Universe within me
5145 I am nourished by the Universe
5146 I choose to extend nourishment to others

Vacation

Vacations are supposed to be relaxing and rejuvenating. Sometimes they don't turn out that way. Ensure that you have exactly the vacation you desire by spending time with conscious self-talk on the subject.

5147 When I go on vacation, I always have a great time
5148 I easily afford any vacation I want to take
5149 I am comfortable in luxurious surroundings
5150 I can easily afford to travel for pleasure
5151 When I travel I always pack just what I need
5152 I keep my good humor at all times when traveling
5153 Airlines always treat my luggage with care
5154 I congratulate myself for taking a vacation this year
5155 My vacations are more luxurious every year
5156 This is the year I take my dream vacation
5157 I remain safe and physically fit my entire vacation
5158 My family and I always agree on vacation choices
5159 This year I find it easier to read and understand maps
5160 Our lodging is perfect for our needs and budget
5161 I like planning and executing my vacation this year
5162 Vacations with my family are calm, relaxed and fun
5163 My budget allows me to take many enjoyable vacations
5164 I deserve a vacation, and I'm planning it now
5165 I deserve to take time off from work, so I do
5166 After vacation, I return to work calm and more focused
5167 My vacation plans go smoothly, with great memories

Weight Challenges

Here's another book, waiting to be written... my experiences with the roller-coaster of weight loss and gain. Do I have it all figured out yet? Nope. Do affirmations help me along the path? Definitely! Use some of the following affirmations to focus on what you want, and don't spend too much time wallowing in what is wrong, for that is all too easy. Be adventurous and decide you are ready to create more successes in this area.

5168 I feel very thin and light-hearted today and always
5169 I choose to be thin and fit
5170 I am continuously and safely melting fat from my body
5171 I love weighing [insert desired number]
5172 I love being a size [insert desired number]
5173 I deserve to weigh [insert desired number]
5174 My weight is quickly returning to its ideal numbers
5175 My figure continues to look as I want it to
5176 I have the proper attitude towards exercise
5177 I have a healthy relationship with food
5178 Today and for the rest of my life, I'm fit
5179 I choose to act like a healthy, fit person
5180 I release excess weight quickly and easily
5181 I choose foods consciously
5182 I consciously choose what I put into my mouth
5183 Eating healthy is natural for me
5184 The numbers on my scales are dropping rapidly
5185 I remain motivated to lose fat
5186 I choose to visualize myself thin and fit today
5187 I love myself now and as I lose weight
5188 I deserve to enjoy eating healthfully
5189 I treat myself well while dieting
5190 My appetite easily stays under control
5191 My muscles respond well to weight training

5192 I have decided to be thin
5193 Every pound I lose is cause for celebration
5194 I release any feelings of being fat or unfit
5195 Nutritious foods are what I prefer
5196 My weight is perfect for my body
5197 Feeling fit is fabulous
5198 Every day I love my body more and more
5199 I release excess weight from all parts of my body
5200 My body prefers healthy food and drink
5201 As my muscles increase, my fat cells deplete
5202 Today I feel my fat melting away
5203 It's okay to have a weight plateau
5204 Each weight plateau I reach, I remain positive
5205 With each pound I lose, I rejoice
5206 I thank God for my weight loss success
5207 It's okay when people compliment my new figure
5208 I enjoy looking at myself in the mirror
5209 Each day my figure is shrinking
5210 My body retains perfect proportions while losing weight
5211 My mind and body communicate better every day
5212 It's okay to lose weight quickly
5213 I'm dedicated to my personal path of fitness
5214 Today is my chance to be healthy
5215 I like shopping for food that's good for me
5216 I easily release my desire for unhealthy foods
5217 I trust the signals my body gives me
5218 I feel hunger only when my body needs food
5219 My appetite is decreasing daily
5220 It's very possible for me to look as I want
5221 I'm motivated to get fit and healthy now
5222 I'm in control of what I eat
5223 What I put in my mouth is up to me
5224 Low-fat foods taste better to me every day
5225 All my organs thank me for my new healthy lifestyle
5226 I continuously find physical activities I enjoy
5227 I deserve to take the time to exercise regularly

5228 I feel my muscles getting stronger
5229 I see more definition in my body daily
5230 I perform isolation exercises frequently today
5231 I take the time to do my yoga today
5232 It's easy for me to find healthy snacks that I love
5233 It's easier to lose weight now that I have positive energy
5234 My body enjoys losing weight and does it very well
5235 My body is firmer now and always
5236 Today I choose to eat as a vegetarian
5237 My body is enjoying the vegetarian lifestyle
5238 God shows me what foods are best to fuel my body
5239 I put food in proper perspective today
5240 Eating meat is part of my past and I release it now
5241 I prefer to eat vegetables and fruits
5242 Eating candy and chocolate is part of my past
5243 Steamed and raw vegetables are appealing to me
5244 As I lose weight, I keep it off
5245 It's okay to be happy and fat
5246 It's okay to be happy and thin
5247 I close my eyes, relax, and see me at goal weight
5248 Today I eat only low-fat foods
5249 I'm free from any desire to eat red meat
5250 I'm now curbing the desire for snacking
5251 I take good care of myself whatever I weigh
5252 My stomach and abdomen continue to shrink daily
5253 My hips and thighs become smaller each day
5254 I feel myself becoming lighter each day
5255 I deserve to lose weight safely and rapidly, and I do
5256 I love all the sizes my body can be
5257 It's exciting to watch my body getting thinner
5258 I quickly attain my body's perfect weight
5259 I always stick to eating a healthy diet
5260 Eating's enjoyable even while cutting fat and calories
5261 My metabolism cooperates in my body to lose weight
5262 It's okay·to be a fat person
5263 It's okay to be a fat person who's becoming thin

5264 Dressing myself is becoming more and more fun
5265 I choose to lose a pound or two a week
5266 I help myself lose weight now by using affirmations
5267 I feel very thin today and always
5268 Today I visualize my body at its optimal weight
5269 It's easy to add fresh fruit and vegetables to my diet
5270 I look great in jeans, and in everything else
5271 I look great naked
5272 My body is cooperating nicely by quickly losing weight
5273 It's okay to remain happy and content with myself
5274 I'm now free from the desire to snack
5275 I let go of any attachments I have to extra body weight

Women

Here is it... the section on "Women" that I promised you. You have to love the first three; don't they just FEEL great when you say them?

5276 I am a Goddess
5277 I am a Princess
5278 I am a Queen
5279 My complexion remains clear and radiant
5280 I look great in little or no make-up
5281 I'm looking younger every day
5282 My female organs function perfectly at all times
5283 I am free of yeast infections
5284 I am free of bladder infections
5285 It's okay for me to possess beauty and brains
5286 It's okay to be a feminist
5287 I am free from breast problems
5288 I have manicures and pedicures regularly
5289 My hormone level is always perfect
5290 I am the most beautiful woman in the Universe
5291 A lunch date with my husband is special to me
5292 I enjoy my femininity
5293 I enjoy being a woman
5294 I join together with all women for a common good
5295 I respect my fellow women
5296 Being a woman makes me happy
5297 It's okay to be a powerful woman
5298 I combine femininity and intelligence beautifully
5299 I'm proud of being a woman
5300 Females are fabulous
5301 I'm a woman who knows what she wants
5302 I accept all positive male and female energy
5303 I accept the essence of my femininity
5304 Women of all shapes and sizes are beautiful
5305 There are plenty of good, decent men in this world

5306 I'm ready now to date men who treat me well
5307 I'm now attracted to nice men
5308 I easily leave behind men who have abused me
5309 I'm now forever free from menstrual cramps
5310 I'm now forever free from what is called PMS
5311 I'm an alive, caring, passionate woman
5312 I'm a very lucky woman
5313 I always remember to take my birth control pill
5314 I now have a wonderful partner in my life
5315 I'm a remarkable woman
5316 I'm a woman of my word
5317 It's an exciting time in history to be a strong woman
5318 It's natural to have women in positions of power
5319 Starting my own business serves humanity well
5320 It's okay to bring femininity to the workplace, it needs it
5321 I'm a very brave, strong woman
5322 It's okay to have a baby out of wedlock
5323 I'm able to comfortably breast feed my baby
5324 It's okay to give my baby up for adoption
5325 I feel honored to birth someone else's child
5326 It's okay to be in love like a school girl
5327 I'm free from feeling I have to act like a big girl
5328 I am free from female-bashing now and always
5329 I am free from male-bashing now and always
5330 I'm grateful to experience life as a woman
5331 I challenge limitations that society has put on women
5332 I support women who choose traditionally male roles
5333 I lay insecurities aside as I plan new projects and goals
5334 I am proud to be a woman and a girl intertwined
5335 I am equally considerate to men and women
5336 Being a woman, I am very strong
5337 I choose to be free forever from breast cancer
5338 I am free forever from uterine and cervical cancer
5339 I'm smart and pretty too
5340 My husband is a remarkable man
5341 My boyfriend is a remarkable man

5342 My girlfriend is a remarkable woman
5343 My partner is a remarkable person
5344 I have an equally high opinion of women and men
5345 I continue using positive affirmations the rest of my life